LANGUAGE ARTS 1100
Teacher's Guide

Author:
Alpha Omega Publications

Editor:
Alan Christopherson, M.S.

Alpha Omega
PUBLICATIONS

804 N. 2nd Ave. E.
Rock Rapids, IA 51246-1759

LANGUAGE ARTS 1100

LIFEPAC® Overview

LANGUAGE ARTS SCOPE & SEQUENCE

KINDERGARTEN

Lessons 1-40

Alphabet
-say the alphabet

Colors
-recognize colors

Directions
-left to right

Following directions
-oral and written

Grammar
-form simple sentences

Listening skills

Personal recognition
-read and write first name
-know age and address
-recognize names of family members

Phonics
-short *a, e, i* vowels
-initial: *b, t, m, r, s, n, d, p, l*
-form and read simple words
-form rhyming words

Shapes
-circle, square, triangle, and rectangle
-recognize shapes in objects

Stories and poems
-create simple stories and poems

Writing
-form circle and lines
-*Aa, Bb, Dd, Ee, Ii, Ll, Mm, Nn, Pp, Rr, Ss,* and *Tt*

Lessons 41-80

Grammar
-sentences begin with capital, end with period

Patterns
-simple shape, color patterns

Personal recognition
-read and write first and last name

Phonics
-short *a, e, i, o,* and *u* vowels
-initial: *k, c, ck, f, h, g, j, v, w, y, z, qu,* and *x*
-read simple sentences

Position/direction concepts
-in/out, in front of/behind, up/down, on/off, open/closed, over/under

Sequencing
-alphabetical order
-simple story

Shapes
-oval

Size concepts
-big/little, large/small

Writing
-*Kk, Cc, Ff, Hh, Oo, Gg, Jj, Vv, Ww, Uu, Yy, Zz, Qq,* and *Xx*

Lessons 81-120

Phonics
-recognize the short vowel sounds
-recognize all initial consonant sounds
-recognize long *a, e, i, o,* and *u* sounds
-silent *e*
-initial consonant digraphs: *sh, ch,* both soft and hard *th*
-final consonant sounds: *_b, _ck, _k, _l*

Word recognition
-color words, number words, and shape words

Writing
-name
-complete alphabet, capital and small letters
-all color words
-number words: *one, two, three, four, five, six*
-shape words: *circle, square, triangle*

Lessons 121-160

Phonics
-recognize the long vowel sounds
-initial consonant digraphs: *wh,* review *ch, sh, th*
-recognize all final consonant sounds

Stories and poems
-create, tell, and recite stories and poems

Word recognition
-position/direction words: *up/down, high/low, in/inside, out/outside, top/bottom*
-number words: *seven, eight, nine, ten*
-shape words: *rectangle, oval, star*

Writing
-number words: *seven, eight, nine, ten*
-shape words: *rectangle, oval, star*
-position/direction words: *up/down, high/low, in/inside, out/outside, top/bottom*

LANGUAGE ARTS SCOPE & SEQUENCE

	Grade 1	Grade 2	Grade 3
UNIT 1	**ALPHABET AND SHORT VOWEL SOUNDS** • Short vowel sounds • Consonants • Main ideas • Rhyming words	**KNOW YOUR NOUNS** • Review vowels & consonants • Beginning, middle, ending sounds • Singular & plural nouns • Common & proper nouns	**OLD AND NEW SKILLS** • Vowels • Consonants • Sentence phrases • Capital letters • Reading skills
UNIT 2	**RHYMING WORDS, ADDING "ING"** • Kinds of sentences • Cardinal & ordinal numbers • Suffixes • Plurals • Classifying	**ACTION VERBS** • Vowel digraphs • Action words – verbs • Following directions • The dictionary • ABC order	**BUILDING WORDS AND SENTENCES** • Vowels – long, short • Questions • ABC order • Capital letters
UNIT 3	**CONSONANT DIGRAPHS, SOFT C AND G** • Consonant digraphs • Compounds • Syllables • Possessives • Contractions • Soft c and g	**SIMPLE SENTENCES** • R-controlled vowels • Consonant blends • Using capital letters • Subjects & verbs in sentences	**WORDS: GETTING TO THE ROOTS** • Root words • Dictionary guide words • Synonyms • Antonyms • Capital letters
UNIT 4	**VERBS, BLENDS, AND SILENT LETTERS** • Paragraphs • Silent letters • Sequencing • Subject-verb agreement	**TYPES OF SENTENCES** • Consonant digraphs • Statement, question, exclamation sentences • Using capital letters • The library	**WORDS: HOW TO USE THEM** • Noun • Verb • Adjective • Adverb • Irregular vowels • Composition
UNIT 5	**LONG VOWELS AND SYLLABLES** • Long vowels • Homonyms • Poetry • Syllables • Possessives • Contractions • Plurals • Suffixes	**USING PUNCTUATION** • Diphthongs • Punctuation review • Using a comma • Rules for making words plural • Writing a biography • Contractions	**SENTENCE: START TO FINISH** • Main idea • Capital letters and punctuation • Paragraphs • Making words plural
UNIT 6	**R-CONTROLLED VOWELS AND PLURALS** • R-controlled vowels • Writing stories • Pronouns • Following directions	**ADJECTIVES** • Rhyming words • Biblical poetry • Adjectives in sentences • Synonyms, antonyms • Thesaurus • Comparative, superlative adjectives	**ALL ABOUT BOOKS** • Main idea • Books • Stories • Poems • Critical thinking
UNIT 7	**VOWEL DIGRAPHS AND SENTENCES** • Vowel digraphs • Letters - business, friendly, invitations • Syllables	**POSSESSIVE NOUNS** • Introduction to letter writing • Pronunciation key • Possessive nouns • Silent consonants • Homonyms	**READING AND WRITING** • For directions • Friendly letters • Pronouns • Fact • Fiction
UNIT 8	**VOWEL DIGRAPHS AND POSSESSIVES** • Vowel digraphs • Subject-verb agreement • Compounds • Contractions • Possessives • Pronouns	**PRONOUNS** • Author's intent & use of titles • Predicting content • Suffixes • Character, setting, & plot • Analogies • Writing in cursive	**READING SKILLS** • For sequence • For detail • Verbs - being, compound • Drama
UNIT 9	**DIPHTHONGS AND CONTRACTIONS** • Vowel digraphs • Titles • Main ideas • Sentences • Paragraphs • Proper nouns	**VERB TYPES AND TENSES** • Review action verbs • Dividing words into syllables • State of being verbs • Past & present verb tenses	**MORE READING & WRITING** • For information • Thank-you letters • Book reports • Reference books
UNIT 10	**PHONICS AND GRAMMAR REVIEW** • Letters and sounds • Contractions • Plurals • Possessives • Sentences • Stories	**PARTS OF SPEECH AND WORD PARTS REVIEW** • Nouns & verbs • Word division • Consonant blends, digraphs • Prefixes, suffixes, root words • Possessives • Pronouns, adjectives	**READING AND WRITING SKILLS REVIEW** • Reading for comprehension • Sentence punctuation • Writing letters • Parts of Speech

LANGUAGE ARTS SCOPE & SEQUENCE

Grade 4	Grade 5	Grade 6	
WRITTEN COMMUNICATION • Word derivations • Story sequence • Writing an outline • Writing a report	STORY MESSAGES • Main idea • Plot • Character • Settings • Dialogue • Diphthong • Digraph	READING FOR A PURPOSE • Critical thinking • Research data • Parables • Synonyms	UNIT 1
SOUNDS TO WORDS • Hard and soft – c and g • Parts of dictionary • Accented syllables • Haiku Poetry	MAIN IDEAS • Poetry • Story • Synonyms • Compounds • Topic sentence • Adjectives • Nouns	FORMING NEW WORDS • Prefixes • Suffixes • Synonyms • Antonyms • Adjectives • Adverbs • Critical thinking	UNIT 2
WORDS: HOW TO USE THEM • Prefixes • Suffixes • Homonyms • Antonyms • Poetry • Stories • Writing an outline	WORDS TO STORIES • Subject • Predicate • Adverbs • Idioms • Critical thinking • Writing a short story	BETTER READING • Story elements • Author's purpose • Information sources • Outline	UNIT 3
MORE WORDS: HOW TO USE THEM • Parts of speech • Possession • Written directions • Verb tenses	WRITTEN REPORT • Outline • Four types of sentences • Metaphor • Simile • Writing the report	SENTENCES • Capitals • Punctuation • Four types of sentences • Author's purpose • Propaganda	UNIT 4
WRITING FOR CLARITY • Figures of speech • Capital letters • Punctuation marks • Writing stories	STORY ELEMENTS • Legend • Implied meaning • Dialogue • Quotations • Word order • Usage • Story elements	READING SKILLS • Following directions • Literary forms • Phrases • Nouns • Verbs • Paragraph structure	UNIT 5
FUN WITH FICTION • Book reports • Fiction • Nonfiction • Parables • Fables • Poetry	POETRY • Rhythm • Stanza • Symbolism • Personification • Irregular plurals	POETRY • Similes • Metaphors • Alliteration • Homonyms • Palindromes • Acronyms • Figures of speech	UNIT 6
FACT AND FICTION • Nouns • Verbs, • Contractions • Biography • Fables • Tall Tales	WORD USAGE • Nouns - common, plural, possessive • Fact • Opinion • Story • Main idea	STORIES • Story elements • Nouns • Pronouns • Vowel digraphs • Business letter	UNIT 7
GRAMMAR AND WRITING • Adjectives to compare • Adverbs • Figurative language • Paragraphs	ALL ABOUT VERBS • Tense • Action • Participles • Of being • Regular • Irregular • Singular • Plural	ANALYZING THE NEWS • Propaganda • News stories • Verbs - auxiliary, tenses • Adverbs	UNIT 8
THE WRITTEN REPORT • Planning a report • Finding information • Outline • Writing a report	READING FLUENCY • Speed reading • Graphic aids • Study skills • Literary forms	READING THE BIBLE • Parables • Proverbs • Hebrew - poetry, prophecy • Bible history • Old Testament law	UNIT 9
COMMUNICATION AND FICTION REVIEW • Reading skills • Nouns • Adverbs • Written communication • Literary forms	STORY ELEMENTS AND POETRY REVIEW • Literary forms • Parts of speech • Writing skills • Study skills	AUTHOR'S PURPOSE REVIEW • Literary forms • Writing letters • Parts of speech • Punctuation	UNIT 10

LANGUAGE ARTS SCOPE & SEQUENCE

	Grade 7	Grade 8	Grade 9
UNIT 1	WORD USAGE • Nouns - proper, common • Pronouns • Prefixes - Suffixes • Synonyms - Antonyms	IMPROVE COMMUNICATION • Roots • Inflections • Affixes • Interjections • Directions – oral, written • Non-verbal communication	STRUCTURE OF LANGUAGE • Nouns • Adjectives • Prepositions • Verbs • Adverbs • Conjunctions • Sentence parts • Diagram sentences
UNIT 2	MORE WORD USAGES • Speech – stress, pitch • Verbs – tenses • Principle parts • Story telling	ALL ABOUT ENGLISH • Origin of language • Classification–nouns, pronouns, verbs, adjectives, adverbs	NATURE OF LANGUAGE • Origin of language • Use – oral and written • Dictionary • Writing a paper
UNIT 3	BIOGRAPHIES • Biography as a form • Flashback technique • Deductive reasoning • Words – base, root	PUNCTUATION AND LITERATURE • Connecting and interrupting • The Essay • Thesis Statement	PRACTICAL ENGLISH • Dictionary use • Mnemonics • Writing a paper • Five-minute speech
UNIT 4	LANGUAGE STRUCTURE • Verbs – tenses • Principle parts • Sentence creativity • Speech – pitch, accent	WORDS • HOW TO USE THEM • Dictionary • Thesaurus • Accents • Diacritical marks • Standard • Nonstandard	READING WITH SKILL • Plot • Setting • Characterization • Conflict • Symbolism
UNIT 5	NATURE OF ENGLISH • Formal • Informal • Redundant expressions • Verb tenses • Subject–verb agreement	CORRECT LANGUAGE USAGE • Using good form • Synonyms • Antonyms • Homonyms • Good speaking qualities	LANGUAGE IN LITERATURE • Collective Nouns • Verbs • Use of comparisons • Gerunds • Participles • Literary genres
UNIT 6	MECHANICS OF ENGLISH • Punctuation • Complements • Modifiers • Clauses – subordinate, coordinate	LANGUAGE AND LITERATURE • History of English • Coordination and Subordination • Autobiography	STRUCTURE AND MEANING IN PROSE AND POETRY • Reading for purpose • Reading for meaning • Reading persuasion • Understanding poetry
UNIT 7	THE HIDING PLACE: A STUDY GUIDE • Sequence of Events • Facts about characters • Author's purpose • Character sketch	CRITICAL READING AND PARAGRAPH SKILLS • Word evaluation • The Paragraph – structure, coherence, introductory, concluding	COMMUNICATION • Planning a speech • Listening comprehension • Letters – business, informal, social
UNIT 8	LITERATURE • Nonfiction • Listening skills • Commas • Semicolons • Nonverbal communication	WRITE • LISTEN • READ • Business letters • Personal letters • Four steps to listen • Nonfiction	THE LIBRARY AND DRAMA • Library resources • Drama – history, elements, reading • *The Miracle Worker*
UNIT 9	COMPOSITIONS • Sentence types • Quality of paragraph • Pronunciation • Nonsense literature	SPEAK AND WRITE • Etymology • Modifiers • Person • Number • Tense • Oral report	STUDIES IN THE NOVEL • History • Define • Write • Critical essay • *Twenty Thousand Leagues Under the Sea*
UNIT 10	GRAMMAR AND NONFICTION REVIEW • Parts of speech • Sentence structure • Punctuation • How to communicate	LANGUAGE ELEMENTS IN REVIEW • Composition structure • Parts of speech • Critical thinking • Literary forms	COMMUNICATION AND LITERATURE REVIEW • Communication – writing, speaking, listening • Using resources • Literature review • Diagram sentences

LANGUAGE ARTS SCOPE & SEQUENCE

Grade 10	Grade 11	Grade 12	
THE DEVELOPMENT OF ENGLISH • Historical development • Varieties of English • Standard English • Changes in English	STANDARD ENGLISH • Need for standard English • Guardians of the standard • Dictionaries • Types of standard English texts	THE WORTH OF WORDS • Word categories • Expository writing • Sentence structure • Diction	UNIT 1
LISTENING AND SPEAKING • Noun plurals • Suffixes • Creating a speech • Nature of listening	WRITING EFFECTIVE SENTENCES • Subordinate – clauses, conjunctions • Relative pronouns • Verbals • Appositives	STRUCTURE OF LANGUAGE • Parts of speech • Sentence Structure • Subordinate Phrases • Subordinate Clauses	UNIT 2
WRITING EFFECTIVE SENTENCES • Verbals • Phrases – prepositional, verbal • Sentence types • Diagram sentences	CLEAR CONNECTIONS: A WRITING WORKSHOP • Understanding pronouns • Using pronouns correctly • Using modifiers correctly • Parallel sentence structures	READ, RESEARCH, AND LISTEN • Reading skills • Resources for research • Taking Notes • Drawing Conclusions	UNIT 3
POWER OF WORDS • Etymology • Connotations • Poetic devices • Poetry – literal, figurative, symbolic	WHY STUDY READING? • Greek and Latin roots • Diacritical markings • Finding the main idea • Analyzing a textbook	GIFT OF LANGUAGE • Biblical origin • Koine Greek • Purpose of Grammar • Semantics	UNIT 4
ELEMENTS OF COMPOSITION • Paragraphs • Connectives • Transitions • Expository writing - elements, ideas	POETRY • Metrical feet • Sets • Musical effects • Universality • Imagery • Connotation	ENGLISH LITERATURE • Early England • Medieval England • Fourteenth century • Chaucer	UNIT 5
STRUCTURE AND READING • Subordinate clauses • Pronouns – gender, case, agreement • Reading for recognition	NONFICTION • Elements • Types – essays, diaries, newspaper, biography • Composition	ELIZABETHAN LITERATURE • Poetry • Prose • Drama • Essay	UNIT 6
ORAL READING AND DRAMA • Skills of oral reading • Drama – history, irony, elements, allegory • *Everyman*	AMERICAN DRAMA • Development • History • Structure • Purpose • *Our Town*	17TH AND 18TH CENTURY LITERATURE • Historical background • Puritan Literature • Common sense – satire • Sensibility	UNIT 7
THE SHORT STORY • Elements • Enjoying • Writing • The Literary Critique	STUDIES IN THE AMERICAN NOVEL • Eighteenth, nineteenth, twentieth Century • *The Old Man and the Sea* • The Critical Essay	CREATIVE WRITING • Fundamentals • Inspiration • Technique and style • Form and process	UNIT 8
THE NOVEL • Elements • *In His Steps* • The Critical Essay • The Book Review	RESEARCH • Stating the thesis • Research • Outline • Writing the paper	ROMANTIC AND VICTORIAN POETRY • Wordsworth • Coleridge • Gordon • Byron • Shelley • Keats • Tennyson • Hopkins • Robert and Elizabeth B. Browning	UNIT 9
COMMUNICATION SKILLS AND FICTION REVIEW • Writing and speech skills • Poetry • Drama • Short stories • Novel	REVIEWING COMMUNICATION SKILLS AND LITERATURE • Analyzing written word • Effective sentences • Expository prose • Genres of American literature	LANGUAGE AND ENGLISH LITERATURE REVIEW • Creative writing • English literature – Medieval to Victorian	UNIT 10

STRUCTURE OF THE LIFEPAC CURRICULUM

The LIFEPAC curriculum is conveniently structured to provide one Teacher's Guide containing teacher support material with answer keys and ten student worktexts for each subject at grade levels 2 through 12. The worktext format of the LIFEPACs allows the student to read the textual information and complete workbook activities all in the same booklet. The easy-to-follow LIFEPAC numbering system lists the grade as the first number(s) and the last two digits as the number of the series. For example, the Language Arts LIFEPAC at the 6th grade level, 5th book in the series would be LAN0605.

Each LIFEPAC is divided into three to five sections and begins with an introduction or overview of the booklet as well as a series of specific learning objectives to give a purpose to the study of the LIFEPAC. The introduction and objectives are followed by a vocabulary section which may be found at the beginning of each section at the lower levels or in the glossary at the high school level. Vocabulary words are used to develop word recognition and should not be confused with the spelling words introduced later in the LIFEPAC. The student should learn all vocabulary words before working the LIFEPAC sections to improve comprehension, retention, and reading skills.

Each activity or written assignment in grades 2 through 12 has a number for easy identification, such as 1.1. The first number corresponds to the LIFEPAC section and the number to the right of the decimal is the number of the activity.

Teacher checkpoints, which are essential to maintain quality learning, are found at various locations throughout the LIFEPAC. The teacher should check 1) neatness of work and penmanship, 2) quality of understanding (tested with a short oral quiz), 3) thoroughness of answers (complete sentences and paragraphs, correct spelling, etc.), 4) completion of activities (no blank spaces), and 5) accuracy of answers as compared to the answer key (all answers correct).

The self test questions in grades 2 through 12 are also number coded for easy reference. For example, 2.015 means that this is the 15th question in the self test of Section 2. The first number corresponds to the LIFEPAC section, the zero indicates that it is a self test question, and the number to the right of the zero the question number.

The LIFEPAC test is packaged at the center of each LIFEPAC. It should be removed and put aside before giving the booklet to the student for study.

Answer and test keys in grades 2 through 12 have the same numbering system as the LIFEPACs. The student may be given access to the answer keys (not the test keys) under teacher supervision so that they can score their own work.

A thorough study of the Scope & Sequence by the teacher before instruction begins is essential to the success of the student. The teacher should become familiar with expected skill mastery and understand how these grade-level skills fit into the overall skill development of the curriculum. The teacher should also preview the objectives that appear at the beginning of each LIFEPAC for additional preparation and planning.

TEST SCORING AND GRADING

Answer keys and test keys give examples of correct answers. They convey the idea, but the student may use many ways to express a correct answer. The teacher should check for the essence of the answer, not for the exact wording. Many questions are high level and require thinking and creativity on the part of the student. Each answer should be scored based on whether or not the main idea written by the student matches the model example. "Any Order" or "Either Order" in a key indicates that no particular order is necessary to be correct.

Most self tests and LIFEPAC tests at the lower elementary levels are scored at 1 point per answer; however, the upper levels may have a point system awarding 2 to 5 points for various answers or questions. Further, the total test points will vary; they may not always equal 100 points. They may be 78, 85, 100, 105, etc.

Example 1

Example 2

A score box similar to ex. 1 above is located at the end of each self test and on the front of the LIFEPAC test. The bottom score, 72, represents the total number of points possible on the test. The upper score, 58, represents the number of points your student will need to receive an 80% or passing grade. If you wish to establish the exact percentage that your student has achieved, find the total points of his correct answers and divide it by the bottom number (in this case 72). For example, if your student has a point total of 65, divide 65 by 72 for a grade of 90%. Referring to ex. 2, on a test with a total of 105 possible points, the student would have to receive a minimum of 84 correct points for an 80% or passing grade. If your student has received 93 points, simply divide the 93 by 105 for a percentage grade of 89%. Students who receive a score below 80% should review the LIFEPAC and retest using the appropriate Alternate Test found in the Teacher's Guide.

The following is a guideline to assign letter grades for completed LIFEPACs based on a maximum total score of 100 points.

Example:

LIFEPAC Test	=	60% of the Total Score (or percent grade)	
Self Test	=	25% of the Total Score (average percent of self tests)	
Reports	=	10% or 10* points per LIFEPAC	
Oral Work	=	5% or 5* points per LIFEPAC	

*Determined by the teacher's subjective evaluation of the student's daily work.

Example:

LIFEPAC Test Score	=	92%	92 × .60	=	55 points
Self Test Average	=	90%	90 × .25	=	23 points
Reports				=	8 points
Oral Work				=	4 points
TOTAL POINTS				=	90 points

Grade Scale based on point system:

100 – 94	=	A
93 – 86	=	B
85 – 77	=	C
76 – 70	=	D
Below 70	=	F

TEACHER HINTS AND STUDYING TECHNIQUES

LIFEPAC activities are written to check the level of understanding of the preceding text. The student may look back to the text as necessary to complete these activities; however, a student should never attempt to do the activities without reading (studying) the text first. Self tests and LIFEPAC tests are never open-book tests.

Language arts activities (skill integration) often appear within other subject curriculum. The purpose is to give the student an opportunity to test his skill mastery outside of the context in which it was presented.

Writing complete answers (paragraphs) to some questions is an integral part of the LIFEPAC curriculum in all subjects. This builds communication and organization skills, increases understanding and retention of ideas, and helps enforce good penmanship. Complete sentences should be encouraged for this type of activity. Obviously, single words or phrases do not meet the intent of the activity, since multiple lines are given for the response.

Review is essential to student success. Time invested in review where review is suggested will be time saved in correcting errors later. Self tests, unlike the section activities, are closed book. This procedure helps to identify weaknesses before they become too great to overcome. Certain objectives from self tests are cumulative and test previous sections; therefore, good preparation for a self test must include all material studied up to that testing point.

The following procedure checklist has been found to be successful in developing good study habits in the LIFEPAC curriculum.

1. Read the introduction and Table of Contents.
2. Read the objectives.
3. Recite and study the entire vocabulary (glossary) list.
4. Study each section as follows:
   a. Read the introduction and study the section objectives.
   b. Read all the text for the entire section, but answer none of the activities.
   c. Return to the beginning of the section and memorize each vocabulary word and definition.
   d. Reread the section, complete the activities, check the answers with the answer key, correct all errors, and have the teacher check.
   e. Read the self test but do not answer the questions.
   f. Go to the beginning of the first section and reread the text and answers to the activities up to the self test you have not yet done.
   g. Answer the questions to the self test without looking back.
   h. Have the self test checked by the teacher.
   i. Correct the self test and have the teacher check the corrections.
   j. Repeat steps a–i for each section.
5. Use the **SQ3R** method to prepare for the LIFEPAC test.
   > **S**can the whole LIFEPAC.
   > **Q**uestion yourself on the objectives.
   > **R**ead the whole LIFEPAC again.
   > **R**ecite through an oral examination.
   > **R**eview weak areas.
6. Take the LIFEPAC test as a closed-book test.
7. LIFEPAC tests are administered and scored under direct teacher supervision. Students who receive scores below 80% should review the LIFEPAC using the **SQ3R** study method and take the Alternate Test located in the Teacher's Guide. The final test grade may be the grade on the Alternate Test or an average of the grades from the original LIFEPAC test and the Alternate Test.

GOAL SETTING AND SCHEDULES

Each school must develop its own schedule, because no single set of procedures will fit every situation. The following is an example of a daily schedule that includes the five LIFEPAC subjects as well as time slotted for special activities.

Possible Daily Schedule

8:15 – 8:25	Pledges, prayer, songs, devotions, etc.
8:25 – 9:10	Bible
9:10 – 9:55	Language Arts
9:55 – 10:15	Recess (juice break)
10:15 – 11:00	Math
11:00 – 11:45	History & Geography
11:45 – 12:30	Lunch, recess, quiet time
12:30 – 1:15	Science
1:15 –	Drill, remedial work, enrichment*

*Enrichment: *Computer time, physical education, field trips, fun reading, games and puzzles, family business, hobbies, resource persons, guests, crafts, creative work, electives, music appreciation, projects.*

Basically, two factors need to be considered when assigning work to a student in the LIFEPAC curriculum.

The first is time. An average of 45 minutes should be devoted to each subject, each day. Remember, this is only an average. Because of extenuating circumstances, a student may spend only 15 minutes on a subject one day and the next day spend 90 minutes on the same subject.

The second factor is the number of pages to be worked in each subject. A single LIFEPAC is designed to take three to four weeks to complete. Allowing about three to four days for LIFEPAC introduction, review, and tests, the student has approximately 15 days to complete the LIFEPAC pages. Simply take the number of pages in the LIFEPAC, divide it by 15 and you will have the number of pages that must be completed on a daily basis to keep the student on schedule. For example, a LIFEPAC containing 45 pages will require three completed pages per day. Again, this is only an average. While working a 45-page LIFEPAC, the student may complete only one page the first day if the text has a lot of activities or reports, but go on to complete five pages the next day.

Long-range planning requires some organization. Because the traditional school year originates in the early fall of one year and continues to late spring of the following year, a calendar should be devised that covers this period of time. Approximate beginning and completion dates can be noted on the calendar as well as special occasions such as holidays, vacations and birthdays. Since each LIFEPAC takes three to four weeks or 18 days to complete, it should take about 180 school days to finish a set of 10 LIFEPACs. Starting at the beginning school date, mark off 18 school days on the calendar and that will become the targeted completion date for the first LIFEPAC. Continue marking the calendar until you have established dates for the remaining nine LIFEPACs making adjustments for previously noted holidays and vacations. If all five subjects are being used, the ten established target dates should be the same for the LIFEPACs in each subject.

TEACHING SUPPLEMENTS

The sample weekly lesson plan and student grading sheet forms are included in this section as teacher support materials and may be duplicated at the convenience of the teacher.

The student grading sheet is provided for those who desire to follow the suggested guidelines for assignment of letter grades as previously discussed. The student's self test scores should be posted as percentage grades. When the LIFEPAC is completed, the teacher should average the self test grades, multiply the average by .25, and post the points in the box marked self test points. The LIFEPAC percentage grade should be multiplied by .60 and posted. Next, the teacher should award and post points for written reports and oral work. A report may be any type of written work assigned to the student whether it is a LIFEPAC or additional learning activity. Oral work includes the student's ability to respond orally to questions which may or may not be related to LIFEPAC activities or any type of oral report assigned by the teacher. The points may then be totaled and a final grade entered along with the date that the LIFEPAC was completed.

The Student Record Book which was specifically designed for use with the Alpha Omega curriculum provides space to record weekly progress for one student over a nine-week period as well as a place to post self test and LIFEPAC scores. The Student Record Books are available through the current Alpha Omega catalog; however, unlike the enclosed forms these books are not for duplication and should be purchased in sets of four to cover a full academic year.

This section of the Language Arts Teacher's Guide also includes a *Book Report Form* and a *Books Read Chart*.

The Book Report Form and the Books Read Chart may be duplicated for individual student use.

WEEKLY LESSON PLANNER

Week of:

	Subject	Subject	Subject	Subject
Monday				
Tuesday	Subject	Subject	Subject	Subject
Wednesday	Subject	Subject	Subject	Subject
Thursday	Subject	Subject	Subject	Subject
Friday	Subject	Subject	Subject	Subject

WEEKLY LESSON PLANNER

Week of:

	Subject	Subject	Subject	Subject
Monday				
Tuesday	Subject	Subject	Subject	Subject
Wednesday	Subject	Subject	Subject	Subject
Thursday	Subject	Subject	Subject	Subject
Friday	Subject	Subject	Subject	Subject

Student Name _____   Year _____

Bible

LP	Self Test Scores by Sections					Self Test Points	LIFEPAC Test	Oral Points	Report Points	Final Grade	Date
	1	2	3	4	5						
01											
02											
03											
04											
05											
06											
07											
08											
09											
10											

History & Geography

LP	Self Test Scores by Sections					Self Test Points	LIFEPAC Test	Oral Points	Report Points	Final Grade	Date
	1	2	3	4	5						
01											
02											
03											
04											
05											
06											
07											
08											
09											
10											

Language Arts

LP	Self Test Scores by Sections					Self Test Points	LIFEPAC Test	Oral Points	Report Points	Final Grade	Date
	1	2	3	4	5						
01											
02											
03											
04											
05											
06											
07											
08											
09											
10											

Student Name _____   Year _____

Math

LP	Self Test Scores by Sections 1	2	3	4	5	Self Test Points	LIFEPAC Test	Oral Points	Report Points	Final Grade	Date
01											
02											
03											
04											
05											
06											
07											
08											
09											
10											

Science

LP	Self Test Scores by Sections 1	2	3	4	5	Self Test Points	LIFEPAC Test	Oral Points	Report Points	Final Grade	Date
01											
02											
03											
04											
05											
06											
07											
08											
09											
10											

Spelling/Electives

LP	Self Test Scores by Sections 1	2	3	4	5	Self Test Points	LIFEPAC Test	Oral Points	Report Points	Final Grade	Date
01											
02											
03											
04											
05											
06											
07											
08											
09											
10											

BOOK REPORT FORM

Title _____   Your Name _____

Author _____   Date _____

Illustrator _____   Main Characters _____

Number of Pages _____   _____

Copyright Date _____   _____

Fiction or Nonfiction _____   Setting _____

Summary:
A summary gives the important events of a story or book. It skips most of the details but a few make the report more interesting. The summary should be written in complete sentences.

_____

_____

_____

_____

_____

_____

_____

_____

_____

_____

_____

_____

_____

Tell why you did or did not like the book.

_____

_____

_____

_____

_____

_____

Name: _____

Books Read			
Title: Author: Date:	Title: Author: Date:	Title: Author: Date:	Title: Author: Date:
Title: Author: Date:	Title: Author: Date:	Title: Author: Date:	Title: Author: Date:
Title: Author: Date:	Title: Author: Date:	Title: Author: Date:	Title: Author: Date:
Title: Author: Date:	Title: Author: Date:	Title: Author: Date:	Title: Author: Date:
Title: Author: Date:	Title: Author: Date:	Title: Author: Date:	Title: Author: Date:
Title: Author: Date:	Title: Author: Date:	Title: Author: Date:	Title: Author: Date:
Title: Author: Date:	Title: Author: Date:	Title: Author: Date:	Title: Author: Date:
Title: Author: Date:	Title: Author: Date:	Title: Author: Date:	Title: Author: Date:
Title: Author: Date:	Title: Author: Date:	Title: Author: Date:	Title: Author: Date:

INSTRUCTIONS FOR LANGUAGE ARTS

The LIFEPAC curriculum from grades 2 through 12 is structured so that the daily instructional material is written directly into the LIFEPACs. The student is encouraged to read and follow this instructional material in order to develop independent study habits. The teacher should introduce the LIFEPAC to the student, set a required completion schedule, complete teacher checks, be available for questions regarding both content and procedures, administer and grade tests, and develop additional learning activities as desired. Teachers working with several students may schedule their time so that students are assigned to a quiet work activity when it is necessary to spend instructional time with one particular student.

Language arts includes those subjects that develop the students' communication skills. The LIFEPAC approach to combining reading, spelling, penmanship, composition, grammar, speech and literature in a single unit allows the teacher to integrate the study of these various language arts subject areas. The variety and scope of the curriculum may make it difficult for students to complete the required material within the suggested daily scheduled time of 45 minutes. Spelling, book reports and various forms of composition may need to be completed during the afternoon enrichment period.

Cursive handwriting is introduced in the second grade LIFEPAC 208 with regular practice following in succeeding LIFEPACs. Diacritical markings are defined in the third grade LIFEPAC 304. A pronunciation key including diacritical markings is provided after the vocabulary word lists in all subjects beginning with LIFEPAC 305.

This section of the Language Arts Teacher's Guide includes the following teacher aids for each unit: Suggested and Required Materials (supplies), Additional Learning Activities, Answer Keys, and Alternate LIFEPAC Tests.

The materials section refers only to LIFEPAC materials and does not include materials which may be needed for the additional learning activities. Additional learning activities provide a change from the daily school routine, encourage the students' interest in learning and may be used as a reward for good study habits.

LANGUAGE ARTS 1101

Unit 1: Standard English

TEACHER NOTES

MATERIALS NEEDED FOR LIFEPAC	
Required	Suggested
(None)	• *World Book Dictionary* or *American Heritage Dictionary* (or any other upper level dictionary) • King James Version (KJV) of the Bible and/or other versions as permitted **Reference materials can be printed, online, or digital formats.*

Language is a tool that needs to be used effectively and responsibly. As Christians, students need to be aware of the impact of their words on others and choose their words accordingly. This LIFEPAC will help students achieve goals through the effective use of language. The ability to distinguish standard English from nonstandard, and to express their needs and desires clearly, will improve the students' ability to communicate and chances for success. The students will also learn in detail about the purpose and use of a dictionary and the methods of research involved in compiling a standard English dictionary.

The teacher should carefully screen any suggested anthologies for unacceptable selections before making them available to the students. Teachers should also be familiar with any suggested student literature to assure that each selection is suitable.

EXTENDED WRITING ASSIGNMENT

For Activity 1.31 the students are to use the questions below to write on a separate sheet of paper two or three paragraphs describing the kind of English they grew up speaking.

1. In what ways is your natural language (daily language) different from Standard English?
2. Did you grow up in the United States? In what region? In a city, a small town, or a rural area?
3. In what ways is your accent different from other regions or from Standard English?
4. What about vocabulary? Think of specific words or phrases that you use that would be considered nonstandard.
5. What aspects of your natural language make it a challenge to learn Standard English?
   Do you speak Standard English at home? Are you learning English as a second language?

Some general notes about grading papers may be helpful. Read the entire paper before marking errors; this reading will give an overall grasp of the student's purpose and method. Many teachers skim the entire class's papers to assess the response to an assignment and to gauge superior and inferior work before assigning an individual grade. Additionally many teachers prefer using a lead pencil instead of red ink or red pencil. Too many corrections tend to discourage or confuse students. Concentrate on one major area of problems (sentence structure, pronouns, or whatever is introduced in the appropriate LIFEPAC) keeping in mind that the writing and communicating effort is a cumulative skill and should be graded as such.

After reading a paper, review the assignment in your mind. Many teachers believe that the completion of an assignment is an average grade—if the student has not addressed the topic assignment, then they are graded poorly or are asked to repeat the assignment. Logic in presenting the assignment, clarity of thought, and precision of word choice are three major considerations to be weighed before assigning a grade. Correct and clear sentence structure, grammatical correctness, appropriate punctuation, and correct spelling should also be considered, with strengths in these areas influencing a higher grade and deficiencies calling for a lower grade. Superior papers should demonstrate superior effort.

The first paper should help locate student weaknesses in expression and organization, as well as in grammar and mechanics. This assignment can provide some ideas about future papers that may be helpful at this point in order to clarify what the student should be working toward. Each paper should have a title and several paragraphs adequately developing the student's ideas. The first paragraph should contain introductory material and the central idea (thesis) to be developed. Each paragraph should then logically develop an aspect of that central idea, an aspect that is usually stated as a topic sentence. The paper should have a definite conclusion; it should not just stop.

After reading the paper through once for content and once for errors, you will be ready to assign a grade. Many teachers give a "content" grade and a "mechanics" grade; others, however, believe that those two aspects should be integrated into a well-written paper. Clarify your own standards, making it known to your students and then being consistent and fair in your grading.

Communication is one of the most important skills available to mankind. To teach students to write well is certainly a challenge. Additionally, to help students learn to explore their own ideas and then to communicate those ideas to other people should be a real pleasure.

ADDITIONAL LEARNING ACTIVITIES

Section 1: Why Standard English?
1. Write sample sentences on the board. Have students identify them as nonstandard or standard. Have volunteers come to the board and rewrite the nonstandard sentences.
2. Discuss these questions with your class.
   a. Do you think people use incorrect English because they do not know better or because they are careless?
   b. What impression do we give to others when we use nonstandard English? Discuss situations where each are acceptable.
   c. Are there situations where you used slang but should not have?
3. Obtain a copy of *The Adventures of Huckleberry Finn* or *The Adventures of Tom Sawyer*. Find some examples of nonstandard or ungrammatical speech. Discuss how you would correctly rewrite these statements.
4. Invite a person who learned English as a second language to visit your class. Have them share some difficulties they experienced in trying to learn the English language. How were they misunderstood? Were some experiences humorous? Embarrassing?
5. Find the song, "Waltzing Matilda," and make a list of the unusual words and meanings in the song (for example, *swagman*). The lyrics can be found online.

6. Obtain a book or digital copies of Shakespearean plays. Write down some examples of English that would appear to be incorrect today.

7. Talk to someone from another country or even another part of the United States. Make a list of words which have a different meaning for the two of you. (For example, do you know what a *turtle hull* is? In West Virginia it is a car trunk.)

Section 2: Dictionaries: Guardians of the Standard

1. Have a dictionary drill. Give a word and see who can stand first and read the definition.

2. Locate as many different types of dictionaries as you can both printed and online (bilingual dictionary, for example). Discuss the differences between each one with the class.

3. If a publishing house is near your town, arrange to take a tour through it. You will see how a book is printed, beginning with the author's manuscript, and then through the editors, layout, proofreaders, printers, and bindery.

4. If Activity 3 is not possible, take a virtual tour of a newspaper plant or print shop.

5. Discuss new words which have entered our vocabulary in the last ten years or less because of new technology, popular culture, and so forth.

6. Have students compare some of the slang used today with some that your parents or grandparents used (far out, cat's meow, groovy, etc.). Does their slang sound funny to you? Does yours sound strange to them? Using a thesaurus, look up words that are commonly overused (such as "good" or "beautiful") and write down a variety of synonyms you could use instead.

7. Have students write down the first name of everyone in your class (or family), then write the meaning of each name by referencing resources online.

Section 3: Varieties of Written Standard English

1. Write a list of roots, prefixes, and suffixes on the board. Ask students to write words containing these affixes and to write their definitions.

2. Find a bill online that is posted by your state legislature. Print enough copies for the class. Compare the English used in these bills with the everyday English we use.

3. Ask students, do you think lawyers, insurance companies, and other business entities should reword their forms so the average person can understand them?

4. Use the list in the first teacher-directed activity. Divide the class into two teams and see who can call out a word first. Then the two teams can have a race looking up the definitions.

5. Have students bring to school some business letters that their parents have received (nothing personal; cut names and addresses off the top and just leave the body of the letter). Pass the letters around and have students make suggestions on how they could be reworded to read better.

6. Instruct students to write a letter or email to a state tourism department, requesting information for a vacation. The request should identify the date they will be there, ask for information about places to see, and ask about the climate for that particular time of the year. The letter or email should be short and to the point.

7. Have students select a favorite poem and copy it on a sheet of paper. At the bottom or on the other side, instruct students to summarize the message and meaning of the poem.

Bible Memory Verses

Section 1
Acts 2:11—the Word of God

Section 2
Philemon 1:6—the effectual communication of faith

Section 3
Job 19:23 and 24—the importance of written communication

Administer the LIFEPAC Test.

The test is to be administered in one session. Give no help except with directions.
Evaluate the tests and review areas where the students have done poorly.
Review the pages and activities that stress the concepts tested.
If necessary, administer the Alternate LIFEPAC Test.

ANSWER KEY

SECTION 1

1.1	natural language acquisition
1.2	telegraphic stage
1.3	holophrastic stage
1.4	overgeneralization
1.5	second language acquisition
1.6	true
1.7	true
1.8	false
1.9	true
1.10	true
1.11	c
1.12	a
1.13	e
1.14	b
1.15	d
1.16	c
1.17	e
1.18	b
1.19	a
1.20	d
1.21	Any order: New England, Southern American, General American
1.22	Any order: regional, social, ethnic
1.23	General American
1.24	Any order: pronunciation, vocabulary, idiomatic expression
1.25	ethnic
1.26	social
1.27	slang, jargon
1.28	c
1.29	a
1.30	b
1.31	Answers will vary. Make sure that the student uses terms like *natural language acquisition*, *dialect*, and *Standard English* in the response.
1.32	b
1.33	d
1.34	e
1.35	f
1.36	c
1.37	a

1.38	false
1.39	false
1.40	true
1.41	true
1.42	true
1.43	b
1.44	c
1.45	a
1.46	Answers will vary. Make sure that the student has included at least three differences between *acquiring* English and *learning* Standard English.
1.47	informal
1.48	formal
1.49	colloquial
1.50	formal
1.51	formal
1.52	colloquial
1.53	informal
1.54	colloquial
1.55	informal
1.56	formal
1.57	Answers will vary. Make sure that the student adjusted the kind of Standard English used to audience and situation.

SELF TEST 1

1.01 c
1.02 b
1.03 d
1.04 a
1.05 b
1.06 c
1.07 e
1.08 a
1.09 b
1.010 d
1.011 false
1.012 true
1.013 true
1.014 true
1.015 false
1.016 true
1.017 false
1.018 true
1.019 true
1.020 false
1.021 a
1.022 b
1.023 a
1.024 b
1.025 b

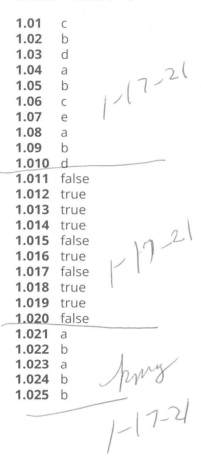

SECTION 2

2.1 f
2.2 c
2.3 h
2.4 e
2.5 j
2.6 k
2.7 g
2.8 b
2.9 d
2.10 i
2.11 a
2.12 Johnson's
2.13 Webster's
2.14 Johnson's
2.15 Johnson's
2.16 Webster's
2.17 Webster's
2.18 Johnson's
2.19 Webster's
2.20 d
2.21 a
2.22 c
2.23 e
2.24 b
2.25 g
2.26 h
2.27 i
2.28 f
2.29 entry word
2.30 respelling
2.31 part of speech
2.32 alternate form
2.33 etymology
2.34 definition
2.35 synonym
2.36 meagre
2.37 alternate forms
2.38 curricula, curriculums
2.39 alternate forms
2.40 *Farther* is considered a variant of *further*. *Farther* should be used when referring to literal distance; *further* should be used in all other senses, especially when referring to figurative distance. Examples: He lives *farther* from work now that he moved. Please consider the matter *further* before making a decision.
2.41 etymology, usage
2.42 to anticipate; to do something before something else happens
2.43 etymology, usage

2.44 several (at least four); answers will vary but could include *beautiful in appearance, dainty, sizable, to some degree or extent, miserable*

2.45 definition, usage

2.46 a. Answers will vary.
Make sure that the student meets the length requirement and lists the dictionaries consulted, including an Internet dictionary, if possible.

b. Answers will vary but should indicate that a shift occurred, away from a "Christocentric" view of truth to a more materialistic one.

SELF TEST 2

2.01 Johnson
2.02 Webster
2.03 Johnson
2.04 Webster
2.05 both
2.06 both
2.07 Johnson
2.08 Webster
2.09 j
2.010 b
2.011 g
2.012 f
2.013 e
2.014 a
2.015 c
2.016 i
2.017 d
2.018 h
2.019 entry word
2.020 respelling
2.021 part of speech
2.022 alternate form
2.023 etymology
2.024 definition
2.025 synonyms
2.026 illustrative quote
2.027 etymology
2.028 definition or usage
2.029 alternate forms
2.030 respelling
2.031 part of speech
2.032 true
2.033 true
2.034 true
2.035 false
2.036 false

SECTION 3

3.1   ordinary
3.2   poetic
3.3   scientific
3.4   technical, scientific
3.5   literary, poetic
3.6   informational, ordinary
3.7   a
3.8   a
3.9   b
3.10   c
3.11   a
3.12   b
3.13   b
3.14   c
3.15   a
3.16   Latin
3.17   Greek
3.18   Old English (writ), Latin (certiorari)
3.19   Old English (writ), Latin (habeas corpus)
3.20   Answers will vary. Make sure that the student has eliminated jargon and broken up larger sentences into smaller ones.
3.21   b
3.22   a
3.23   d
3.24   c
3.25   a
3.26   a
3.27   c
3.28   b
3.29   a
3.30   d
3.31   poetry and prose
3.32   poetry and prose
3.33   poetry
3.34   prose
3.35   poetry and prose
3.36   d
3.37   e
3.38   c
3.39   b
3.40   a
3.41   a house
3.42   Passage 1 includes a brief literal description of two houses, predominantly their foundations.
Passage 2 includes extensive description of a literal house.
Passage 3 treats the house completely figuratively, using its features to describe a person's (dead) body.

3.43   Passage 1 uses the image of building a house as a point of comparison (analogy) to illustrate a point about the results of listening to or rejecting Christ's words.
3.44   The house is the setting of Passage 2. Its condition is linked to the mental state of its owner ("the perfect keeping of the character of the premises with the accredited character of the people"). The ancient, weather-worn house with a "barely perceptible fissure" in its walls foreshadows the doom of Roderick Usher. (Both, by the end of the story, are destroyed.)
3.45   In Passage 3 the poet uses the house as a metaphor of the human body.
"Life and thought" were the occupants, but they have abandoned the house (i.e., the person died). The "windows" are the eyes; the "door" is the mouth. The reference to the house being "builded of the earth" reminds the reader that mankind was made from the dust of the ground. Life and thought are now occupying a new house, the "mansion" in heaven described in the last stanza.
3.46   All three texts use the image and features of a house in order to make important points about human existence.
3.47   Passage 1 is closest to ordinary language. As a sermon, it uses a conversational tone, traditional sentence structure, and little figurative language.
3.48   Passage 3 is a poem built around the metaphor of the body as a house. Structurally, it makes use of regular meter (trochaic tetrameter), rhyme (*abba*, *cddc*, *effe*, *ghhg*, *ijji*), stanzas (five), and other features characteristic of poetry.
3.49   Answers will vary. Make sure that the student follows the length requirements and applies what he or she has learned in Section 3 to this assignment.

SELF TEST 3

3.01	scientific
3.02	poetic
3.03	ordinary
3.04	technical
3.05	informational
3.06	literary
3.07	technical
3.08	literary
3.09	informational
3.010	literary
3.011	literary
3.012	informational
3.013	technical
3.014	technical
3.015	informational
3.016	c (medical journals are technical texts)
3.017	b
3.018	e
3.019	b
3.020	a
3.021	a
3.022	b
3.023	d
3.024	c
3.025	e

LIFEPAC TEST

1. h
2. e
3. g
4. k
5. n
6. p
7. c
8. f
9. l
10. m
11. a
12. j
13. d
14. i
15. b
16. o
17. f
18. h
19. e
20. a
21. c
22. i
23. d
24. g
25. b
26. entry word
27. respelling
28. alternate form
29. etymology
30. definition
31. synonym
32. illustrative quote
33. scientific
34. poetic
35. ordinary
36. technical
37. informational
38. literary

39. Sample Essay (100–200+ words)

Human beings are prewired for language. As infants we begin to learn language as the direct result of hearing it, not as a result of formal instruction. The process, called natural language acquisition, moves through a series of distinct developmental stages ending in basically adult-level language use in pronunciation and vocabulary in as soon as five years. The learner's language is profoundly influenced by language environment, including factors such as geographical region, ethnicity, and social grouping, all of whose characteristics shape the speaker's language use in distinct ways.

Mastery of Standard English, on the other hand, requires formal instruction. The focus is on getting everyone to use a single variety of English in public settings for sake of clear communication. Students must learn rules for how to pronounce and spell words and use them in sentences. They must learn how to speak and write English following specific forms and levels of formality, depending on the occasion and audience. They must learn how to read a variety of Standard English texts for a variety of purposes. Mastery of Standard English is an important mark of education and is expected of employees in the workplace and in a variety of other public settings.

ALTERNATE LIFEPAC TEST

1. false
2. false
3. true
4. true
5. true
6. false
7. true
8. false
9. false
10. true
11. g
12. l
13. f
14. a
15. c
16. j
17. e
18. h
19. b
20. d
21. alternate form
22. respelling
23. etymology
24. usage
25. entry word
26. scientific
27. poetic
28. ordinary
29. technical
30. Answers will vary; examples include law books, academic journals, research reports
31. literary
32. Answers will vary; examples include sermons, essays, speeches, short stories, novels, poetry
33. informational
34. Answers will vary; examples include contracts, warranties, user guides, policies, instructions

35. Sample Essay (100–200+ words)

Samuel Johnson's *A Dictionary of the English Language* was the largest, most authoritative dictionary of the English language at the time it was written during the mid-eighteenth century. The dictionary reflected the grammarian tradition of which Johnson was a part. For Johnson, lexicography was an effort to preserve the English language from corruption and change. The "pure" language he documented was that of the educated elite at court and the universities as well as the greatest authors of English literature up to his time. The words, definitions, and examples he included represented a prescriptive approach to language. That is, his dictionary documented the grammarians' perspective concerning how the language should be used.

A generation or two after the publication of Johnson's dictionary, Noah Webster produced *The American Dictionary of the English Language*. Webster made extensive use of Johnson's work in his own but expanded on his methods in some important ways. First, while using Johnson's historical method, Webster also included word etymology as an important part of his definitions. He also consulted a much broader segment of the educated populace and even included colloquial terms rather than restricting his usage models to the few elite. In using these methods, Webster took the first steps toward a more descriptive approach to language in which language is documented according to how it is actually used.

LANGUAGE ARTS 1101

ALTERNATE LIFEPAC TEST

NAME _____

DATE _____

SCORE _____

Answer *true* **or** *false* (each answer, 2 points).

1. _____ Jargon is a kind of dialect.

2. _____ Prose never makes use of figurative language.

3. _____ A word's history is its etymology.

4. _____ Simile is a kind of figurative language.

5. _____ Descriptive, Prescriptive, and Historical are three methods used in lexicography.

6. _____ Legalese is a type of slang.

7. _____ Poetry often uses imagery.

8. _____ Formal Standard English and Standard English are the same thing.

9. _____ Slang is acceptable in formal Standard English.

10. _____ Both first and second language learners over-generalize.

Match the type of language to the correct example (each answer, 2 points).

11. _____ informational text

12. _____ colloquial English

13. _____ technical text

14. _____ formal Standard English

15. _____ jargon

16. _____ regional dialect

17. _____ literary text

18. _____ informal Standard English

19. _____ slang

20. _____ English as a second language

a. By the power invested in me as a minister of the Gospel, I now pronounce you man and wife. What God has joined together, let not man put asunder.

b. So, they tied the knot. Cool!

c. Open the guestbook one-half hour before the ceremony. After the vows are said, lead the bridal party to the receiving line.

d. I happy for you!

e. Entreat me not to leave thee or to refrain from following after thee. For whither thou goest I will go.

f. The aforementioned parties, in entering into said Agreement, hereby mutually swear that they have, to the best of their abilities, provided a truthful representation of their intent …

g. To register online at Smith's Bridal, complete the form below and press "Enter."

h. Congratulations, Jim and Sarah. We're very happy for you. Thank you for inviting us.

i. Way to go, guys! You'll do great!

j. Ya'll make a fine couple! I reckon you'll be happy.

Indicate which part of a dictionary entry you would use to find the item requested (each answer, 4 points).

21. _____ the past tense form of "prove" (*proved* or *proven*?)

22. _____ the syllable structure of *pusillanimous*

23. _____ the source language of *phlebotomy*

24. _____ the difference between *affect* and *effect*

25. _____ the primary (preferred) spelling of *judgement/judgment*

Label the parts of the diagram below. Each number references the element immediately following it (each answer, 3 points).

① _____ Language   ② _____ Language

③ _____ Language

④ _____ Texts   ⑥ _____ Texts   ⑧ _____ Texts

⑤ _____ Example   ⑦ _____ Example   ⑨ _____ Example

26. _____ ①   27. _____ ②

28. _____ ③   29. _____ ④

30. _____ ⑤   31. _____ ⑥

32. _____ ⑦   33. _____ ⑧

34. _____ ⑨

Essay (this answer, 10 points).

35. On a separate sheet of paper, explain the difference between Johnson's and Webster's approach to lexicography and how their methods represent the difference between a prescriptive and descriptive approach to language.

   Use the following terms in your essay: *historical method, etymology, prescriptive, descriptive.* (100–200 words)

LANGUAGE ARTS 1102

Unit 2: Writing Effective Sentences

TEACHER NOTES

MATERIALS NEEDED FOR LIFEPAC	
Required	Suggested
(None)	• *World Book Dictionary* or *American Heritage Dictionary* • King James Version (KJV) of the Bible and/or other versions as permitted • any American Literature text which the student is currently using **Reference materials can be in printed, online, or digital formats.*

The abilities to speak and to write effectively are two of the most important skills learned in school. Ideas, however good, are of little importance unless they can be expressed clearly. Understanding the way language works and the ways it can be used is indispensable to developing language skills. In this LIFEPAC, students will study main clauses and subordinate clauses. They will learn how clauses are used correctly in writing and will study such subordinating devices as relative pronouns, subordinating conjunctions, and verbals. Students will also learn to form and to use participles, gerunds, infinitives, and appositives. This LIFEPAC will help students to understand and to communicate God's Word more effectively.

EXTENDED WRITING ASSIGNMENT

Since no "Extended Writing Assignment" has been provided in this LIFEPAC, assign the one listed under "Additional Activities" in Section 1. For basic grading guidelines, refer to the Language Arts 1101 section of this Teacher's Guide, "Extended Writing Assignment."

ADDITIONAL LEARNING ACTIVITIES

Section 1: Clauses

1. Write clauses on the board and have students identify each as either main clause or subordinate clause. If it is a subordinate clause, ask for suggestions to finish the sentence.

2. Write the beginning of a sentence on the board. Have students complete with a noun clause, adverb clause, or adjective clause.

3. Divide the students into groups. Assign each student a "name"—noun, verb, adverb, adjective, noun clause, and so on. Have each write a word or clause fitting student's "name," then choose other students to form a sentence with each. Some humorous sentences should result from this activity, as the students will not know the words the others wrote down until they form a line.

4. This is the "Extended Writing Assignment." Assign it at the beginning of the LIFEPAC study and collect it before students take the LIFEPAC Test. See Extended Writing Assignment in the Language Arts 1101 teacher notes for grading guidelines. Students are to read the story of the Good Samaritan that is in Mark 10:30–37 and write the story in their own words to include the theme for today. Students are to identify all verbals, appositives, relative pro-nouns, and subordinating conjunctions. Select some of the best-written assignments to share with the class.

5. Assign students to find two examples of each of the following clauses in any literature book: main clause, subordinate clause, noun clause, adjective clause, or adverb clause.

6. Have students find two examples of the preceding clauses in their Bible.

Section 2: Subordinating Devices

1. Write a sentence on the board using subordinating conjunctions. Have students tell you the use, place, time, reason, condition, purpose, result, or comparison of the conjunctions.

2. Write a series of short sentences on the board. (Example: John lost his patience.) Have the students add a subordinate clause to each sentence, positioning some at the beginning of sentences and some at the end.

3. Write a series of pairs of sentences on the board. (Example: She finished singing. There were tears in her eyes.) Have students combine the pairs of sentences by making one of the sen-tences a subordinate clause.

4. Have students work together or independently to collect quotations from famous people. Tell them to identify clauses and other parts of speech. (Do all of these quotations use cor-rect English?)

5. Assign students to write a short story, and identify the subordinating conjunctions and their uses.

6. Have students go through a newspaper and cut out an article on current events, sports, and so forth. Create a class color code so that students can underline various clauses and iden-tify them.

Section 3: Verbals and Appositives

1. Write sentences on the board and leave blanks for the students to fill in gerunds or gerund phrases.

2. Write pairs of sentences on the board. Have the students combine sentences by reducing one of them to a gerund phrase.

3. Do these same two exercises (1 and 2) with infinitive phrases.

4. Write several sets of four or five short related sentences on the board. Have students com-bine each of the sets into a single, well-written sentence.

5. Tell partners to select three paragraphs from an American literature text. Have them look for examples of the various constructions you have studied in this section. Discuss the way these varied constructions add interest.

6. Have students write an interesting paragraph on one of these topics:
   a. songbirds common to the Midwest or other geographic region
   b. athletic training for spiritual growth
   c. who is my "neighbor"

   Have partners exchange papers in order to underline and identify the constructions studied in this LIFEPAC. Provide time for them to discuss both paragraphs.

7. Beginning readers' books use short sentences. ("Dick saw Jane. See Jane run.") Find a beginning reading book. Have students rewrite one or two pages, connecting the sentences and adding adjectives, clauses, and so forth to make one or two well-written sentences or paragraphs.

8. Have students draw several cartoons with captions, illustrating one of the constructions in this section. To check the parts of speech, ask a question about the cartoon that will need an answer of a participle or other part of speech. (Example: cartoon of girl or boy drying dishes and some broken dishes on the floor. Caption reads, "The broken dishes were lying on the floor." Ask yourself the question, "Which dishes?" Answer, "The broken dishes." (The word *broken* is a participle.)

9. Have students look through some old magazines, newspapers, and comic strips to find ten examples of verbals. Instruct them to paste these examples on paper and explain under each clipping how each verbal is used.

Bible Memory Verses

Section 1
Ecclesiastes 1:17—example of compound-complex sentence

Section 2
Ecclesiastes 9:11—example of a relative pronoun
Ecclesiastes 4:9—example of subordinate conjunctions

Section 3
Psalm 50:2—example of an appositive

Administer the LIFEPAC Test.

The test is to be administered in one session. Give no help except with directions.
Evaluate the tests and review areas where the students have done poorly.
Review the pages and activities that stress the concepts tested.
If necessary, administer the Alternate LIFEPAC Test.

ANSWER KEY

SECTION 1

1.1 My brother attends Notre Dame University.

1.2 Have you seen my pet turtle,

1.3 Most of the juniors and all of the seniors will be going

1.4 Cats make good house pets, I like dogs

1.5 Cathy went, we were out of milk.

1.6 Although the assignment was given early,

1.7 when an oil rig in the North Sea exploded.

1.8 While industrial pollution continues to be a problem,

1.9 that established Federal control over strip-mined land.

1.10 when it was conducting a study of work environments,

1.11 although the proposal met with some opposition.

1.12 as the President formulated his position on labor unions and strikes.

1.13 who hired illegal aliens.

1.14 which had been dumped into the city water system

1.15 if the United States wishes to perform more successfully in international competition.

1.16 S

1.17 OP

1.18 DO

1.19 SC

1.20 S

1.21 OP

1.22 DO

1.23 SC

1.24 S

1.25 DO

1.26 SC

1.27 DO

1.28 that she made, suggestions

1.29 who is a Christian, Charles Colson

1.30 whom I had not seen for several years, cousins

1.31 that sits on top of the hill, house

1.32 which was to him the most beautiful dog in the world, dog

1.33 that I told you about, novel

1.34 which her mother has given her, those

1.35 who was sitting close to them, gentleman

1.36 whose horse we borrowed, man

1.37 that I recommended, product

1.38 When you obey your parents, you please the Lord. please

1.39 Although he spends much time playing tennis, he manages to get his studying done. manages

1.40 Please get to bed early since you have a test tomorrow. get

1.41 The picnic was postponed because the rain ruined the grounds. was postponed

1.42 He is ready to go whenever he is called. is ready

1.43 Since the advertisements are sometimes misleading, it is important to read the labels. important

1.44 You may go as soon as you have finished the test. may go

1.45 Tim will not eat the food unless you taste it first. will (not) eat

1.46 The girls greeted each other as though nothing had happened. greeted

1.47 The guide tied the canoe to a tree so that it could not float away. tied

1.48 adverb

1.49 adverb

1.50 noun

1.51 adverb

1.52 adjective

1.53 adverb

1.54 noun

1.55 adverb

1.56 adjective

1.57 adverb

1.58 noun

1.59 adverb

1.60 adverb

1.61 adverb

1.62 noun

1.63 Example:
one of the things I can depend on

1.64 Example:
who was caught

1.65 Example:
which we played yesterday

1.66 Example:
What I do with my money

1.67 Example:
whenever he could

1.68 Example:
whatever suspicious activity I see

1.69 Example:
I borrowed

1.70 Example:
what I like to do best

1.71 Example:
which carried five adults

1.72 Example:
after the guests had assembled

1.73 Example:
What I'm trying to do is to finish my homework.

1.74 Example:
He told me that he had been to town.

1.75 Example:
Melissa reads her poetry to whoever will listen.

1.76 Example:
His fingerprints prove that he is not the thief.

1.77 Example:
The girl who sits next to me has a dress like mine.

1.78 Example:
Do you know whether the book that was torn has been mended?

1.79 Example:
The neighbor whose window I broke is letting me mow her lawn to repay her.

1.80 Example:
This is the park that I mentioned in my letter.

1.81 Example:
After I practice my clarinet. I can go to the movie.

1.82 Example:
I read that book when I was in seventh grade.

1.83 Example:
He can't go skiing because he broke his leg.

1.84 Example:
Jennifer didn't buy the watch because she couldn't afford it.

SELF TEST 1

1.01 adverb

1.02 main

1.03 adjective

1.04 noun

1.05 noun

1.06 subordinate

1.07 adverb

1.08 Any order:
a. noun
b. adjective
c. adverb

1.09 Most of the teachers are Americans, though a few come from England and France.
adverb

1.010 When school opens in the fall, students are happy to rejoin their friends.
adverb

1.011 We believe that Christianity is the key to a better world.
noun

1.012 The prince's chief interest was tennis, which he was just learning to play.
adjective

1.013 After we have read the story, we will talk about it.
adverb

1.014 If people are going to respect authority when they grow up, they must learn how when they are young.
adverb

1.015 When I joined them in the waiting room for a cup of tea, they seemed pleased.
adverb

1.016 The orphan did not wish to be adopted by the American family that had asked for him.
adjective

1.017 Andris was an orphan who had barely survived in a war camp.
adjective

1.018 America needs young people who are loyal and industrious.
adjective

1.019 What Scripture tells us
subject

1.020 whoever plays best.
object of preposition

1.021 what I was looking for in my purse.
direct object

1.022 that I had failed to set the alarm.
subject complement

1.023 That I was in a hurry
subject

1.024 <u>which she borrowed yesterday</u>.
book

1.025 <u>who found the money</u>
boy

1.026 <u>which had disappeared</u>.
toy

1.027 <u>whose portrait hangs on the wall</u>.
woman

1.028 <u>which come to the feeder</u>
birds

1.029 <u>when school is out</u>.
will pick up

1.030 <u>as rapidly as road conditions would permit</u>.
drove

1.031 <u>as any person I know</u>.
talented

1.032 <u>more quickly than I did</u>.
finished

1.033 <u>although he had been warned not to touch
the hot stove</u>.
burned

SECTION 2

2.1 who

2.2 whoever

2.3 whom

2.4 whoever

2.5 whomever

2.6 whoever

2.7 who

2.8 whom

2.9 whom

2.10 whom

2.11 Hint: *Whomever* must function as an object in the clause.
Example: Invite whomever you wish.

2.12 Hint: *Whoever* must function as the subject of a clause.
Example: We will elect whoever is best qualified.

2.13 Example: What is important is not who wins but how he plays.

2.14 Example:
I did not know whom I was addressing.

2.15 Example:
Psalm 100 is one which I have memorized.

2.16 Example:
The red dress is the one that Tom likes to see me wear.

2.17 Example:
I like what you have written so far.

2.18 a. Example:
After you finish reading that book, I'd like to read it.
b. time

2.19 a. Example:
I've heard of the author, although I haven't read his books.
b. condition

2.20 a. Example:
I can throw the ball as far as you can.
b. comparison

2.21 a. Example:
He looked as if he had just run a race.
b. comparison

2.22 a. Example:
My mother gave me a key so that I would not be locked out.
b. purpose

2.23 a. Example:
You don't have to go just because I asked to.
b. reason

2.24 a. Example:
Wipe your feet before you come in.
b. time

2.25 a. Example:
If you've finished washing dishes, I'll help you with your homework.
b. condition

2.26 a. Example:
Since you've already heard that song, I'll play another one.
b. reason

2.27 a. Example:
We want to start early so you can get there as soon as you can.
b. time

2.28 a. Example:
I can work faster than you can.
b. comparison

2.29 a. Example:
Though we were friends, we never told each other secrets.
b. condition

2.30 a. Example:
I can't order the banner for the gymnasium unless everyone contributes.
b. condition

2.31 a. Example:
Parents can't wait until they buy their new car.
b. time

2.32 a. Example:
I will come to the picnic when I get home from church.
b. time

2.33 a. Example:
My grandmother visits us whenever she can.
b. time

2.34 a. Example:
She can never remember where she left her glasses.
b. place

2.35 a. Example:
This dog follows me wherever I go.
b. place

2.36 a. Example:
Dad called while you were gone.
b. time

2.37 a. Example:
The teacher alphabetized the vocabulary words in order that we could look them up faster.
b. condition

SELF TEST 2

2.01 relative pronouns
2.02 adverb
2.03 Either order:
a. adjective
b. noun
2.04 subordinate
2.05 whose
2.06 whom
2.07 noun
2.08 noun
2.09 noun
2.010 that
2.011 which
2.012 who
2.013 whose
2.014 whom
2.015 until
2.016 Although
2.017 Whenever
2.018 Because
2.019 before
2.020 true
2.021 true
2.022 false
2.023 true
2.024 false
2.025 false
2.026 true
2.027 true
2.028 true
2.029 false
2.030 (Whenever I feel depressed)
adverb
2.031 (who had not studied his lessons)
adjective
2.032 (whose car was dented)
adjective
2.033 (What I told you)
noun
2.034 (which held the clean sheets)
adjective
2.035 Whom
2.036 whom
2.037 who
2.038 whom
2.039 whom
2.040 who
2.041 whom
2.042 which
2.043 whose
2.044 who

SECTION 3

3.1 a. feeling
     b. felt
3.2 a. riding
     b. ridden
3.3 a. smoking
     b. smoked
3.4 a. praying
     b. prayed
3.5 a. kneeling
     b. knelt
3.6 a. sacrificing
     b. sacrificed
3.7 a. stealing
     b. stolen
3.8 a. talking
     b. talked
3.9 a. hitting
     b. hit
3.10 a. freezing
      b. frozen
3.11 Example:
My brother owns a stable of riding horses.
3.12 Example:
On my wall is a picture of a praying child.
3.13 Example:
The talking children could not hear the teacher.
3.14 Example:
Freezing weather kills tender plants
3.15 Example:
Be sure to douse that smoking campfire.
3.16 Example:
The horse, ridden hard, was sweating.
3.17 Example:
Frozen dinners are convenient, if not very tasty.
3.18 Example:
The stolen car was returned to its owners.
3.19 Example:
Hit by the ball, the runner went to first base.
3.20 Example:
Smoked herring is not my idea of a treat.
3.21 think
     a. Example: Thinking is hard work.
     b. subject
3.22 climb
     a. Example: My daughter likes climbing trees.
     b. direct object
3.23 give
     a. Example: The greatest pleasure is giving.
     b. subject complement

3.24 prepare
     a. Example: I helped by preparing dinner.
     b. object of preposition
3.25 Example:
to help the student
3.26 Example:
to reach the East by sailing west
3.27 Example:
to have a Coke
3.28 Example:
to hurry you
3.29 Example:
to worry about the test
3.30 a. Kimberly touched the flowers to see if they were real.
     b. adverb
3.31 a. We sprayed our yard to eliminate all the mosquitoes.
     b. adverb
3.32 a. Always keep receipts to prove that you have paid your bills.
     b. adverb
3.33 a. To put your elbows on the table is bad manners.
     b. noun
3.34 a. I have a job to complete before I can draw my pay.
     b. adjective
3.35 a. We are planning a party to honor our Seniors.
     b. adjective
3.36 a. The committee sent out cards to remind members of the meeting.
     b. adverb
3.37 the Scoutmaster
Mr. Murray
3.38 my youngest sister
Mary
3.39 a popular senior
president
3.40 one of our favorite charities
Salvation Army
3.41 the book by Charles Colson
Born Again
3.42 a. Example:
The wounded man smiled grimly.
     b. man
     c. Example:
He looked out at the pouring rain.
     d. rain

3.43 a. Example:
　　　　　Don't you like my singing?
　　　　b. direct object
　　　　c. Example:
　　　　　Writing poetry is my hobby.
　　　　d. subject

3.44 a. Example:
　　　　　To know him is to love him.
　　　　b. subject-subjective complement
　　　　c. Example:
　　　　　It's a sin to tell a lie.
　　　　d. subjective complement

3.45 a. Example:
　　　　　My brother, the minister, is in town.
　　　　b. brother
　　　　c. Example:
　　　　　Mrs. Jones, this is my neighbor, Tom.
　　　　d. neighbor

3.46 a. to catch
　　　　b. infinitive

3.47 a. flattering
　　　　b. participle

3.48 a. fining
　　　　b. participle

3.49 a. to save
　　　　b. infinitive

3.50 a. roaring
　　　　b. gerund

3.51 a. dropping
　　　　b. gerund

3.52 a. crying
　　　　b. gerund

3.53 a. doings
　　　　b. gerund

3.54 a. to eat
　　　　b. infinitive

3.55 a. babbling
　　　　b. gerund

3.56 a. goings
　　　　b. gerund

3.57 a. sweeping
　　　　b. participle

3.58 a. to erase the boards
　　　　b. me

3.59 a. subject
　　　　b. to speak

3.60 a. "To do thy will"
　　　　b. will

3.61 a. participle
　　　　b. adjective

3.62 a. appositive
　　　　b. (may) roam

3.63 a. phrase
　　　　b. speaker

3.64 a. adjective
　　　　b. Dr. Black

3.65 a. participle phrase
　　　　b. participle

3.66 a. participle
　　　　b. judge

3.67 Teacher check

SELF TEST 3

3.01 because our house was too small
  a. adverb
  b. subordinating conjunction
3.02 that were dead
  a. adjective
  b. relative pronoun
3.03 Why anyone should believe this rumor
  a. noun
  b. neither
3.04 the children enjoyed
  a. adjective
  b. neither
3.05 when the whistle blew
  a. adverb
  b. subordinating conjunction
3.06 which he had just bought
  a. adjective
  b. relative pronoun
3.07 until you finish your homework
  a. adverb
  b. subordinating conjunction
3.08 whose
3.09 whom
3.010 which
3.011 who
3.012 whom
3.013 whoever
3.014 whom
3.015 what
3.016 whichever
3.017 whom
3.018 adverb
3.019 adjective (or noun)
3.020 subordinate
3.021 whose
3.022 possessive
3.023 Running up the stairs
  he
3.024 standing near the cookie jar
  me
3.025 destroyed by fire
  house
3.026 Seizing the weapon from the intruder
  he

3.027 suffering from malnutrition
  refugees
3.028 serving others
  OP
3.029 Driving carelessly
  S
3.030 forming the dough into loaves of bread
  SC
3.031 flying to Bermuda for vacation
  DO
3.032 telling his mother
  OP
3.033 To win an argument
  S
3.034 to succeed as an architect
  Adj
3.035 to avoid facing the truth
  DO
3.036 to learn new ideas from his experiments
  Adv
3.037 to point out your responsibilities as a
  Christian student
  DO
3.038 Feeling my inability to do anything in my own
  strength
  a. participle
  b. infinitive
3.039 Charmed by her gracious manner
  excited
  a. participle
  b. participle
3.040 To obey
  to hearken
  a. infinitive
  b. infinitive
3.041 the circus animal trainer
  tapping her trunk
  a. appositive
  b. gerund
3.042 fascinated by the clown
  to leave the circus tent
  a. participle
  b. infinitive

LIFEPAC TEST

1. The Mason-Dixon line, which is perhaps the most famous border ever established by surveying methods, has been designated a National Historic Civil Engineering Landmark.
   adjective

2. When the Little Red Schoolhouse began to give way to the "consolidated school" in the 1920's, one of the problems was transportation.
   adverb

3. It is not right to make a promise unless one is sure he can fulfill the promise.
   adverb

4. After school I retrieved my boots from under the bridge where I had hidden them in the morning on my way to school.
   adverb

5. The man who wrote this new and popular book autographed copies of it at the bookstore.
   adjective

6. DO
7. SC
8. OP
9. S
10. S
11. automobile
    Example:
    which had been driven 100,000 miles,
12. beggar
    Example:
    who went to the Salvation Army shelter
13. grades
    Example:
    which you have received
14. apple
    Example:
    that I gave to the teacher
15. tree
    Example:
    whose branches had died
16. comes unless she is ill.
17. better after she has taken the medicine.
18. attractive as any I have seen.
19. carry whenever I go to the store.
20. better than he did last year.
21. We like him as much as we like them.
22. We like him as much as they like him.

23. Any ten; any order:
    a. although
    b. since
    c. after
    d. because
    e. before
    f. if
    g. than
    h. though
    i. unless
    j. whenever
    (as)
    (as if)
    (as soon as)
    (until)
    (where)
    (wherever)
    (while)
    (when)
24. story that
25. box what
26. man who
27. child whose
28. manager whom
29. victim whoever
30. a. hiding   b. hidden
31. a. chewing   b. chewed
32. a. beginning   b. begun
33. a. thinking   b. thought
34. gerund
35. participle
36. participle
37. Camping outdoors
    a. gerund   b. noun (subject)
38. frightened by the siren,
    a. participle
    b. adjective (modifies *Alice*)
39. going
    a. gerund
    b. object of preposition
40. To reject cheap entertainment
    a. infinitive   b. noun (subject)
41. living in poverty
    a. participle
    b. adjective (modifies *artist*)
42. a nocturnal hunter,
43. the giant water reed which the Egyptians used to manufacture writing material
44. outlaw brother of Jesse James,

ALTERNATE LIFEPAC TEST

1. participle
2. infinitive
3. appositive
4. three
5. gerund
6. appositive
7. elliptical
8. which was to be delivered in unmarked five-dollar bills
   a. adjective
   b. (ten thousand) dollars
9. After he had waited an hour
   a. adverb
   b. received
10. that ran between two commercial buildings near the downtown area
    a. adjective
    b. alley
11. as if they had been perfect strangers
    a. adverb
    b. boarded
12. that they could outsmart the law
    a. adjective
    b. belief
13. Any order:
    a. subject
    b. subject complement
    c. direct object
    d. object of preposition
14. adverb
15. noun
16. noun
17. adjective
18. adverb
19. a. talking
    b. reading
    c. running
    d. sleeping
    e. swimming
20. a. dealt
    b. cheated
    c. run
    d. praised
    e. written
21. a. to learn
    b. to draw
    c. to pray
    d. to stimulate
    e. to starve
22. who; circle *man*
23. whom; circle *man or woman*
24. whom; circle *artist*
25. gerund
26. participle
27. participle
28. gerund
29. a. infinitive
    b. participle
30. gerund
31. gerund
32. infinitive
33. participle
34. Any order:
    a. after
    b. although
    c. as
    d. as if
    e. so that
    f. because
    g. before
    h. if
    i. since
    j. as soon as
    or than, though, unless, until, when, whenever, where, wherever, while, or in order that

LANGUAGE ARTS 1102

ALTERNATE LIFEPAC TEST

NAME _____

DATE _____

SCORE _____

Complete these statements (each answer, 3 points).

1. A verb form which ends in *-ing, -d, -ed, -n, -en,* or *-t,* and is used as an adjective is called a(n) _____ .

2. Formed by the word *to* and a verb, a(n) _____ may be used as a noun, adjective, or adverb.

3. A noun or pronoun that renames another noun or pronoun nearby in the sentence, and is usually separated by commas, is called a(n) _____ .

4. We have studied _____ (how many) kinds of verbals.

5. A verbal which ends in *-ing* and is used as a noun is called a(n) _____ .

6. A noun or pronoun that identifies or explains the noun or pronoun which preceded it is called a(n) _____ .

7. A clause in which one or more words are understood but omitted is called a(n) _____ clause.

Underline each subordinate clause, identify it as an *adjective* clause or an *adverb* clause, and list the word or phrase it modifies (each sentence, 3 points).

	Kind of Clause	Word it Modifies

8. The note repeated the telephone demand for ten thousand dollars, which was to be delivered in unmarked five-dollar bills.
    a. _____ b. _____

9. After he had waited an hour, Mr. Jones received a telephone call directing him to go at once to a certain motel room.
    a. _____ b. _____

10. There he was instructed to go to an alley that ran between two commercial buildings near the downtown area.
    a. _____ b. _____

11. At six o'clock Jones and the police officers boarded the bus as if they had been perfect strangers.
    a. _____ b. _____

12. Three criminals, filled with greed, had entered a conspiracy in the mistaken belief that they could outsmart the law.
    a. _____ b. _____

Complete this activity (each answer, 2 points).

13. List the four uses of noun clauses.

    a. _____ b. _____

    c. _____ d. _____

Identify each italicized clause as a *noun* clause, an *adjective* clause, or an *adverb* clause (each sentence, 2 points).

14. "We must plan a picnic for the holiday," said Mrs. Bailey, *while the children were getting dressed*.
    _____

15. The instructor decided *that this girl must have inherited her father's musical ability*.
    _____

16. He saw *how eager she was to do her best*.
    _____

17. Searching for something *that she could wear*, Sally pulled open the drawer in the dresser.
    _____

18. The child offered resistance *when the hair brush pulled her long curls*.
    _____

Write the correct verb form (each answer, 1 point).

19. gerunds

    a. talk _____

    b. read _____

    c. run _____

    d. sleep _____

    e. swim _____

20. past participles

    a. deal _____

    b. cheat _____

    c. run _____

    d. praise _____

    e. write _____

21. infinitives

    a. learn _____

    b. draw _____

    c. pray _____

    d. stimulate _____

    e. starve _____

Underline the correct relative pronoun and circle the noun or pronoun to which it relates (each sentence, 2 points).

22. The modernistic sculpture in the shopping center was designed by a man (which / who) had received training in design in Europe.

23. The Award for Excellence in Architectural Design will go to the man or woman (who / whom) the committee selects.

24. Renoir is an artist (who / whom) most people admire.

Identify each italicized word as a *gerund*, a *participle*, or an *infinitive* (each answer, 2 points).

25. Daily *jogging* is a good way to build one's strength and stamina.

    _____

26. There was the kite, *dangling* from the telephone wires.

    _____

27. *Anticipating* the taste of the food, Father sat down at the table and carefully adjusted his napkin.

    _____

28. *Wishing* will never make your dreams come true.

    _____

29. The neighbors began (a) *to look* for a new house, (b) *hoping* to find a quieter neighborhood.

    a. _____

    b. _____

30. The thief confessed to *stealing* the camera from the display. _____

31. Your *telling* me what you heard doesn't disturb me at all. _____

32. The Christian desires *to be* godly rather than rich. _____

33. The children went to sleep *dreaming* of the party. _____

Complete this list (each answer, 1 point).

34. List ten subordinating conjunctions which may be used to introduce clauses.

   a. _____   b. _____   c. _____   d. _____

   e. _____   f. _____   g. _____   h. _____

   i. _____   j. _____

LANGUAGE ARTS 1103

Unit 3: Clear Connections: A Writing Workshop

TEACHER NOTES

MATERIALS NEEDED FOR LIFEPAC	
Required	Suggested
(None)	• *World Book Dictionary* or *American Heritage Dictionary* • King James Version (KJV) of the Bible and/or other versions as permitted *Reference materials can be in printed, online, or digital formats.*

Clear communication is among the most important skills taught in school. One way to improve verbal and written skills is by analyzing sentences and examining their components. Part of this LIFEPAC focuses upon one of those components—the pronoun—and suggests ways of solving pronoun reference and agreement problems. The second half of this LIFEPAC is composed of ways to identify and correct common sentence errors by working with phrases and clauses.

EXTENDED WRITING ASSIGNMENT

Before taking Self Test 3, write a two- to three-paragraph essay, using all eight classes of pronouns. Underline and label one example of each type. Include in your essay at least one sentence containing parallel structure. Underline the parallel elements and identify their grammatical type. Include at least one sentence with an introductory modifying phrase that is related to the rest of the sentence that follows.

ADDITIONAL LEARNING ACTIVITIES

Section 1: Understanding Pronouns

1. Divide the class in half. Have a student from each team go to the board. Have them write the answer as you drill students on the pronoun information presented in Section 1. Students at their desks may complete the exercise on separate sheets of paper.

2. Have students write a brief (one paragraph) narration, telling about a recent experience. Students may share these paragraphs with other students. Now have the students rewrite their paragraphs, omitting all personal pronouns. This exercise readily points up the advantages of using pronouns.

3. Have students keep a log for several days, recording instances of incorrect pronoun usage in newspapers, magazines, on the radio, and other public media.

Section 2: Using Pronouns

1. Have students look over a previously graded paper, trying to locate instances of pronoun reference and agreement. Students may circle the appropriate pronoun, then draw an arrow to its reference.

2. Have students exchange short papers (perhaps the extended writing project from another LIFEPAC) and look for pronoun errors of reference and agreement.

3. Students may keep a record of pronoun errors found in their own writing. (Limit this project to a week or two to prevent it from becoming tedious; students who consistently make this sort of error will quickly find which pronouns they need to restudy.)

Section 3: Writing Strong Sentences

1. Using printed or online anthologies, students should locate a teacher-selected prose passage. Within that passage direct the students to identify prepositional phrases, adverb and adjective clauses, and verbal phrases. If students can identify proper sentence structure, they are more likely to use sentence structure appropriately.

2. With students working in pairs, have them devise five sentences, each with a construction error (split infinitive, dangling modifiers such as participles, gerunds, infinitives, and elliptical clauses; see Section 3 of the LIFEPAC).

3. Have each partner correct the five sentences written for the previous activity.

4. Students may add a section to their "error logs" by recording instances of incorrect constructions found in mass printings.

Bible Memory Verses

Section 1
Psalm 23:1—example of possessive case
Psalm 23:1—example of nominative case
Psalm 23:2—example of objective case

Section 2
Psalm 91:2—example of clear reference in using pronouns

Section 3
Ecclesiastes 3:1–8—example of parallel structure and proper modifier

Administer the LIFEPAC Test.

The test is to be administered in one session. Give no help except with directions.
Evaluate the tests and review areas where the students have done poorly.
Review the pages and activities that stress the concepts tested.
If necessary, administer the Alternate LIFEPAC Test.

ANSWER KEY

SECTION 1

1.1	b		**1.43**	second
1.2	g		**1.44**	plural
1.3	a		**1.45**	masculine
1.4	c		**1.46**	nominative
1.5	f		**1.47**	reflexive
1.6	e		**1.48**	intensive
1.7	d		**1.49**	reciprocal
1.8	h		**1.50**	personal
1.9	S		**1.51**	indefinite
1.10	IO		**1.52**	interrogative
1.11	DO		**1.53**	demonstrative
1.12	POS		**1.54**	relative
1.13	OP		**1.55**	interrogative
1.14	PN		**1.56**	demonstrative
1.15	APP			
1.16	SG			
1.17	I			
1.18	you			
1.19	him			
1.20	theirs			
1.21	his			
1.22	she			
1.23	third			
1.24	singular			
1.25	feminine			
1.26	nominative			
1.27	their			
1.28	third			
1.29	plural			
1.30	NONE			
1.31	possessive			
1.32	them			
1.33	third			
1.34	plural			
1.35	NONE			
1.36	objective			
1.37	theirs			
1.38	third			
1.39	plural			
1.40	NONE			
1.41	possessive			
1.42	you			

SELF TEST 1

1.01 f
1.02 i
1.03 d
1.04 j
1.05 a
1.06 k
1.07 g
1.08 c
1.09 h
1.010 b
1.011 e
1.012 l
1.013

Nominative Case		
Person	**Singular**	**Plural**
first	I	we
second	you	you
third	he, she, it	they

Objective Case		
Person	**Singular**	**Plural**
first	me	us
second	you	you
third	him, her, it	them

Possessive Case		
Person	**Singular**	**Plural**
first	my, mine	our, ours
second	your, yours	your, yours
third	his, her, hers, its	their, theirs

1.014 everybody, S, IND
1.015 himself, none, INN
1.016 that, S, REL
1.017 whom, DO, INT
1.018 herself, DO, REF
1.019 his, POS or SG, P
1.020 each other, OP, REC
1.021 that, S, DEM
1.022 he, S, P
1.023 it, IO, P
1.024 he, PN, P
1.025 I, S (or AP), P

SECTION 2

2.1 me
2.2 me
2.3 she
2.4 he
2.5 them
2.6 Answers will vary. See 2.3 and 2.4 as nominative examples; 2.1, 2.2, and 2.5 as objective examples.
2.7 we
2.8 us
2.9 us
2.10 we
2.11 we
2.12 Answers will vary: See 2.7 for a nominative example and 2.8 for an objective example.
2.13 she
2.14 me
2.15 they
2.16 they
2.17 he
2.18 Answers will vary. See 2.13 for a *than* example and 2.14 for an *as* example.
2.19 our
2.20 her
2.21 us
2.22 me
2.23 him
2.24 Answers will vary. See 2.19 for an example.
2.25 Answers will vary. See 2.23 for an example.
2.26 whom
2.27 whom
2.28 whose
2.29 who
2.30 who
2.31 Answers will vary. See 2.26 for an example.
2.32 Answers will vary. See 2.27 for an example.
2.33 ambiguous
2.34 remote
2.35 broad, ambiguous
2.36 broad
2.37 broad
2.38 broad
2.39 remote
2.40 broad, ambiguous
2.41 ambiguous
2.42 broad
2.43 ambiguous

(**2.44 through 2.64**: Answers will vary. The revision should address the **bolded** selection.)

2.44   Original: When Jill picked up Nancy on the way to the game, **she** said she had forgotten the tickets.

         Revision: When Jill picked up Nancy on the way to the game, Nancy said she had forgotten the tickets.

2.45   Original: We drove to the doctor's office only to find out that **they** were closed for the day.

         Revision: We drove to the doctor's office only to find out that the office was closed for the day.

2.46   Original: If a car accident happens and **you** leave the scene before the police arrive, **it** is a crime.

         Revision: Leaving the scene of a car accident before the police arrive is a crime.

2.47   Original: Jason received a *National Geographic* subscription for Christmas, **which** is his favorite magazine.

         Revision: For Christmas, Jason received a subscription to *National Geographic*, which is his favorite magazine.

2.48   Original: Over the summer Frank learned a lot about installing and repairing computers. In fact, **it** changed his career path.

         Revision: Over the summer Frank learned a lot about installing and repairing computers. In fact, his summer experience changed his career path.

2.49   Original: We need new tires. I'm sure **this** is why **it** shudders when we drive on the freeway.

         Revision: We need new tires. I'm sure their condition explains why the car shudders when we drive on the freeway.

2.50   Original: After I read Dickens's *The Tale of Two Cities*, **he** became my favorite author.

         Revision: After I read *The Tale of Two Cities*, Dickens became my favorite author.

2.51   Original: We decided to enjoy a walk to the park after eating supper. **This** became a regular habit.

         Revision: We decided to enjoy a walk to the park after eating supper. This walk became a regular habit.

2.52   Original: Since the car leaks oil on the driveway, put a piece of cardboard under **it**.

         Revision: Since the car leaks oil on the driveway, put a piece of cardboard under the car to catch the drops.

2.53   Original: If a person has income tax questions, the IRS can help **you** with **it**.

         Revision: The IRS can help out any person who has income tax questions.

2.54   Original: Joe always knew it was time to feed his fish when **he** started blowing bubbles.

         Revision: Joe always knew it was time to feed his fish when the fish started blowing bubbles.

2.55   Original: Every good **homeowner** plays **his** part in keeping the neighborhood clean and safe. (or Every good homeowner/ his or her)

         Revision: All good homeowners play their part in keeping neighborhoods clean and safe.

2.56   Original: The **club** decided to hold **their** annual bake sale in the church gym.

         Revision: The club decided to hold its annual bake sale in the church gym.

2.57   Original: **The boys** always ends up hurting **himself** in our soccer games.

         Revision: The boys always ends up hurting themselves in our soccer games.

2.58   Original: **No one** managed to find **his** way to the cabin until after dark.

         Revision: None of the hikers managed to find their way to the cabin until after dark.

2.59   Original: **Some** of the pieces of the game found **its** way under the couch.

         Revision: Some of the pieces of the game found their way under the couch.

2.60 Original: The **students and their class president** gave his teacher an award.

Revision: The students and their class president gave their teacher an award.

2.61 Original: Neither **the director nor the editor** gives its permission to print the article.

Revision: Neither the director nor the editor gives their permission to print the article.

2.62 Original: I could tell that either **the clarinetists or the violinists** didn't know **his or her** music very well.

Revision: I could tell that either the clarinetists or the violinists didn't know their music very well.

2.63 Original: Is this the same **committee that are** planning to endorse the new candidate?

Revision: Is this the same committee that is planning to endorse the new candidate?

2.64 Original: **One** of the girls on the front row left **their** purse under the chair.

Revision: One of the girls on the front row left her purse under the chair.

SELF TEST 2

2.01	d
2.02	a
2.03	c
2.04	e
2.05	f
2.06	b
2.07	her
2.08	who
2.09	he
2.010	us
2.011	we
2.012	me
2.013	she
2.014	us
2.015	us
2.016	his
2.017	their
2.018	whom, who
2.019	whom
2.020	whom
2.021	whose
2.022	whose
2.023	his or her
2.024	his

(**2.025 through 2.037**: Answers will vary. The revision should address the **bolded** selection.)

2.025 Original: When **Shelly** called her **sister**, she told **her** about the new baby.

Revision: Shelly called her sister and told her about the new baby.

2.026 Original: Since the **roof** leaks on the family room **floor**, we need to repair **it**.

Revision: We need to repair the roof, since it leaks on the family room floor.

2.027 Original: Hurricane Katrina devastated the Gulf Coast. **This** exposed weaknesses in the Federal Emergency Management Administration.

Revision: Hurricane Katrina devastated the Gulf Coast. This tragedy exposed weaknesses in the Federal Emergency Management Administration.

2.028 Original: **They** say that the internet is becoming more popular than television.

Revision: Media analysts say that the Internet is becoming more popular than television.

2.029 Original: **Mr. Davis's** students found **him** to be smart, kind, and firm.

Revision: Mr. Davis's students found their teacher to be smart, kind, and firm.

2.030 Original: The street was full of potholes, but we learned **they** would be repairing it.

Revision: The street was full of potholes, but we learned street crews would be repairing it.

2.031 Original: Every **voter** must take the time **he** need to understand the issues.

Revision: Every voter must take the time he or she needs to understand the issues.

2.032 Original: A taxpayer must either know the law or find **himself** an accountant.

Revision: Taxpayers must either know the law or find themselves accountants.

2.033 Original: The **team** washed **its** uniform after removing **it** from storage.

Revision: The team washed their uniforms after removing them from storage.

2.034 Original: **The girls** should know **her** way around the library by now.

Revision: The girls should know their way around the library by now.

2.035 Original: For your information, the gate has been locked, should **anyone** try to make **his** way through.

Revision: For your information, the gate has been locked, should prowlers try to make their way through.

2.036 Original: Some of the **noodles has** made **its** way into the pudding mix.

Revision: Some of the noodles have made their way into the pudding mix.

2.037 Original: The **soldiers and their platoon leader** plans to take leave to visit **his** family.

Revision: The soldiers and their platoon leader plan to take leave to visit their families.

SECTION 3

(**3.1 through 3.20**: Answers will vary. The revision should address the **bolded** selection.)

3.1 MM

Original: We planned **to in three years or less, take** a trip to Asia.

Revision: We planned to take a trip to Asia in three years or less.

3.2 MM

Original: Philip **scarcely** had read three chapters when he found out the library book was overdue.

Revision: Philip had read scarcely three chapters when he found out the library book was overdue.

3.3 SM

Original: Samantha said **during winter break** she would write a letter to the pastor.

Revision: Samantha said she would write a letter to the pastor during winter break.

or   During winter break, Samantha said she would write a letter to the pastor.

3.4 DM

Original: **Trimming back the deadwood**, the rose bush bloomed beautifully in the spring.

Revision: After I trimmed back the deadwood, the rose bush bloomed beautifully in the spring.

3.5 MM

Original: We were so hungry that we **almost** ate the whole pizza.

Revision: We were so hungry that we ate almost the whole pizza.

3.6 MM

Original: I found out they were planning to feed me dessert **while I ate my supper**.

Revision: While I ate my supper I found out they were planning to feed me dessert.

3.7 MM

Original: **Searching busily through the drawer**, the antique pendant was finally found by the worried girl.

Revision: Searching busily through the drawer, the worried girl finally found the antique pendant.

3.8   SM
   Original: Shelly said **frequently** she needed to leave early to get to work on time.
   Revision: Shelly frequently said she needed to leave early to get to work on time.
   or   Shelley said she frequently needed to leave early to get to work on time.

3.9   MM
   Original: Tom found the memory box for the baby **on the dusty closet shelf**.
   Revision: Tom found the baby's memory box on the dusty closet shelf.

3.10   DM
   Original: **Having read the children a bedtime story**, the house was shut down for the night.
   Revision: Having read the children a bedtime story, I shut the house down for the night.

3.11   Original: Marsha's plan was **to practice** every day for the recital, **to work** on trouble spots in the music, and **arrive** at the concert hall early to steady her nerves.
   Revision: Marsha's plan was to practice every day for the recital, to work on trouble spots in the music, and to arrive at the concert hall early to steady her nerves.

3.12   Original: John's choice was either **to rescue** the bird or **allowing** it to fend for itself.
   Revision: John's choice was either to rescue the bird or to allow it to fend for itself.

3.13   Original: The hikers knew **that the hike** was six miles, **that it usually required** the entire day, and **to start** after 10:00 a.m. would not be wise.
   Revision: The hikers knew that the hike was six miles, that it usually required the entire day, and that a start time

of any later than 10:00 a.m. would not be wise.

3.14   Original: Jefferson was **both the writer** of the Declaration of Independence **and he was** the nation's third president.
   Revision: Jefferson was both the writer of the Declaration of Independence and the nation's third president.

3.15   Original: These days getting a good job depends almost as much **on who one knows** as **to have knowledge** in your field.
   Revision: These days getting a good job depends almost as much on who one knows as on what one knows.

3.16   Original: We found the dessert both **delicious** and **filled us up**.
   Revision: We found the dessert both delicious and filling.

3.17   Original: **A hot meal, a warm bed,** and **resting for two days** rejuvenated the weary traveler.
   Revision: A hot meal, a warm bed, and two days rest rejuvenated the weary traveler.

3.18   Original: Good writing requires **knowing** your purpose, **knowing** your audience, **and to have** an organizational plan.
   Revision: Good writing requires knowing your purpose, knowing your audience, and having an organizational plan.

3.19   Original: **Not only** was Jill very ill from lack of sleep, **she was** malnourished from a poor diet.
   Revision: Not only was Jill very ill from lack of sleep, but she was also malnourished from a poor diet.

3.20   Original: Today we could go **on a picnic, for a long drive**, or **walk** to the park.
   Revision: Today we could go on a picnic, for a long drive, or on a walk to the park.

3.21   Answers will vary.

SELF TEST 3

3.01   d
3.02   c
3.03   e
3.04   b
3.05   a
3.06   MM
3.07   MM
3.08   DM
3.09   FP
3.010   MM
3.011   FP
3.012   SM
3.013   MM
3.014   DM
3.015   MM
3.016   SM
3.017   MM

(**3.018 through 3.029**: Answers will vary. The revision should address the **bolded** selection.)

3.018   Original: The rescue team **almost** arrived too late.
        Revision: The rescue team arrived almost too late.

3.019   Original: He knew what to **hardly** say.
        Revision: He hardly knew what to say.

3.020   Original: **Twisting the valve tightly shut**, the fire hydrant stopped spewing water into the street.
        Revision: When the workers twisted the valve tightly shut, the fire hydrant stopped spewing water into the street.

3.021   Original: The scientist received high marks **for his brilliance** and **because he was humorous**.
        Revision: The scientist received high marks for his brilliance and humor.

3.022   Original: **While gathering fish out of his net**, a sea urchin stung the fisherman.
        Revision: While gathering fish out of his net, the fisherman was stung by a sea urchin.

3.023   Original: We enjoyed his company **because of his stories** and **how he told them**.
        Revision: We enjoyed his company because of his stories and his story telling.

3.024   Original: Mary noticed **sometimes** her hair was askew.
        Revision: Mary noticed her hair was askew sometimes.

3.025   Original: Admitting that he was partially at fault, the driver tried **to not completely avoid** taking blame.
        Revision: Admitting that he was partially at fault, the driver tried not to completely avoid taking blame.

Note: Allowing *completely* to continue to split the infinitive prevents the ambiguity that would arise in saying ...*the driver tried not to avoid completely taking blame*. One meaning emphasizes his partial avoidance, the other his partial acceptance.

3.026   Original: **While playing basketball in the driveway**, my ball was punctured by a cactus.
        Revision: While I was playing basketball in the driveway, my ball was punctured by a cactus.

3.027   Original: **Baring his teeth and growling**, the mailman edged nervously away from the dog.
        Revision: The mailman edged nervously away from the dog, which was baring its teeth and growling.

3.028   Original: Dad said **on the way to the game** we would stop for ice cream.
        Revision: Dad said we would stop for ice cream on the way to the game.

3.029   Original: Dillan tried to sweep the messy leaves from the roof **with the broom**.
        Revision: Dillan tried to use the broom to sweep the messy leaves from the roof.

LIFEPAC TEST

1. g
2. d
3. h
4. c
5. b
6. f
7. i
8. j
9. k
10. a
11. e
12. anyone, IND, S
13. his, P, SG
14. this, DEM, S
15. which, INT, S
16. him, P, DO
17. itself, REF, DO
18. me
19. us
20. we
21. they
22. us
23. his
24. who's
25. whom
26. whom
27. she

(**28 through 37**: Answers will vary. The revision should address the **bolded** selection.)

28. REF
    Original: After **Jeff** talked to his **brother** about the project, **he** went home.
    Revision: Jeff went home after he talked to his brother about the project.

29. AGR
    Original: Every frugal **shopper** counts **their** coupons before **they** shop.
    Revision: All frugal shoppers count their coupons before they shop.

30. AGR
    Original: **Someone** decided to leave **their** mess behind for others to clean up.
    Revision: Someone decided to leave a mess behind for others to clean up.

31. REF
    Original: The crowd sat through two hours of rainy soccer. **It** ended in a tie.
    Revision: The crowd sat through two hours of rainy soccer. The game ended in a tie.

32. AGR
    Original: Neither the Smiths nor **Mr. Paulson** remembered to purchase **their** hunting license.
    Revision: Neither the Smiths nor Mr. Paulson remembered to purchase his hunting license.

33. FP
    Original: **Knowing his tendency** to oversleep and **because he needed** to be on time, Paul bought an alarm clock.
    Revision: Knowing his tendency to oversleep and knowing he needed to be on time, Paul bought an alarm clock.

34. DM
    Original: **After mopping the floor**, the house was ready for guests.
    Revision: After Traci mopped the floor, the house was ready for guests.

35. SM
    Original: The general told his orderly **before the battle** he could go on leave.
    Revision: Before the battle the general told his orderly he could go on leave.

36. MM
    Original: We kept an extra rack for the stove **in the closet**.
    Revision: In the closet we kept an extra rack for the stove.

37. MM
    Original: Our driving instructor taught us to **confidently but not aggressively** drive.
    Revision: Our driving instructor taught us to drive confidently but not aggressively.

ALTERNATE LIFEPAC TEST

1. himself, REF, DO
2. one another, REC, IO
3. himself, INT, NONE
4. yours, P, PN
5. who, REL, S
6. his, P, POS
7. e
8. i
9. f
10. a
11. h
12. c
13. d
14. g
15. b
16. l
17. j
18. me
19. we
20. I
21. us
22. us
23. your
24. whose
25. who
26. who
27. her

(**28 through 37**: Answers will vary. The revision should address the **bolded** selection.)

28. REF
   Original: For dessert, Mother served ice cream with nuts on top, **which** delighted us.
   Revision: Mother served a delightful dessert of ice cream with nuts on top.

29. REF
   Original: **Fred's** ideas were great, so we asked **him** to write them down for us to ponder.
   Revision: Fred had great ideas, so we asked him to write them down for us to ponder.

30. AGR
   Original: Either the camp director or his **assistant** will make **their** appearance at the fundraiser.
   Revision: Either the camp director or his assistant will make his appearance at the fundraiser.

31. AGR
   Original: Can **anyone** recite **his** life's verse?
   Revision: Can anyone recite his or her life's verse?

32. REF
   Original: When I stopped by the post office, **they** were closed.
   Revision: When I stopped by the post office, the building was closed.

33. FP
   Original: Sally was grateful for **a meal on her table**, **a roof over her head**, and **that family loved her**.
   Revision: Sally was grateful for a meal on her table, a roof over her head, and the love of her family.

34. MM
   Original: **With his loud roar**, the zookeeper was hesitant to feed the lion.
   Revision: The zookeeper was hesitant to feed the lion with his loud roar.

35. SM
   Original: My mother said **occasionally** she suffers from migraine headaches.
   Revision: My mother said she occasionally suffers from migraine headaches.

36. MM
   Original: Because of the flat tire, we **nearly** arrived three hours late.
   Revision: Because of the flat tire, we arrived nearly three hours late.

37. FP
   Original: **Knowing** what to do is one thing, but **to do it** is quite another.
   Revision: Knowing what to do is one thing, but doing it is quite another.

LANGUAGE ARTS 1103

ALTERNATE LIFEPAC TEST

NAME _____

DATE _____

SCORE _____

Underline the pronoun in each sentence. Identify the noun function and class of each pronoun in the blanks provided. Use the abbreviations below in your answers. For intensive pronouns, put **NONE** for noun function (each question, 3 points).

Noun Function		Pronoun Class	
subject	**S**	personal	**P**
direct object	**DO**	interrogative	**INT**
indirect object	**IO**	relative	**REL**
predicate nominative	**PN**	demonstrative	**DEM**
object of preposition	**OP**	reflexive	**REF**
appositive	**AP**	intensive	**INN**
subject of gerund	**SG**	indefinite	**IND**
possessive noun	**POS**	reciprocal	**REC**

Example:

____S____ ____P____ You need to choose the right pronoun.

1. _____ _____ The maestro seated himself and began a piano concerto.

2. _____ _____ The club members gave one another gifts at the Christmas party.

3. _____ _____ The senator himself came to the political rally.

4. _____ _____ The large pile of lost-and-found items is yours.

5. _____ _____ The day was busy for Mrs. Larkin, who kept a booth at the farmer's market.

6. _____ _____ Samuel fell asleep over his book.

Match the vocabulary term to its definition (each answer, 1 point).

7. _____ reflexive pronoun

8. _____ compound antecedent

9. _____ interrogative pronoun

10. _____ demonstrative pronoun

11. _____ collective noun

12. _____ person

13. _____ case

14. _____ relative pronoun

15. _____ reference

16. _____ squinting modifier

17. _____ split infinitive

a. a pronoun that points out a particular person or thing

b. the relationship between a pronoun and its antecedent

c. the form of a pronoun indicating the person speaking, person spoken to, or person or thing spoken about

d. the grammatical relationships between words in a sentence and the forms of words used to communicate those relationships (in English, nominative, objective, and possessive are case forms for nouns and pronouns)

e. a self-pronoun that acts as an indirect or direct object and moves the action of the verb back on the subject

f. a pronoun used in asking a question

g. a pronoun that introduces a relative clause and references the element modified

h. a singular noun naming a collection or group

i. two or more nouns and/or pronouns serving the same grammatical function and followed by a pronoun that references one or all nouns

j. a verbal form containing interrupting modifiers between to and the verb

k. the principal that words, phrases, and clauses joined by conjunctions need to be of the same grammatical type

l. a word, phrase, or clause that logically modifies more than one element in the sentence, producing ambiguity

Underline the correct pronoun in each sentence (each answer, 2 points).

18. John and David drove behind Samuel, Jason, and (I / me) on the way to the game.

19. Because (we / us) students tended to procrastinate, the teacher tracked our progress closely.

20. Wanting the victory as much as (I / me), Phil went all out in the fourth quarter.

21. Making fudge for the Smiths and (we / us) was an annual ritual for our neighbors.

22. Father decided to tell (we / us) kids about his retirement plan.

23. We really appreciated (you / your) dropping by this afternoon.

24. (Who's / Whose) are those keys on the desk?

25. Reagan is the president (who / whom) helped bring the Berlin Wall down.

26. (Who / Whom) should run that errand for Mrs. Johnson?

27. What an honor it was to have the pastor visit the family and (she / her) at the hospital.

Identify the error in each sentence as a problem in pronoun reference (REF) or pronoun agreement (AGR). Then, rewrite each sentence (each question, 5 points).

28. _____ For dessert, Mother served ice cream with nuts on top, which delighted us.

_____

_____

29. _____ Fred's ideas were great, so we asked him to write them down for us to ponder.

_____

_____

30. _____ Either the camp director or his assistant will make their appearance at the fundraiser.

_____

_____

31. _____ Can anyone recite his life's verse?

_____

_____

32. _____ When I stopped by the post office, they were closed.

_____

_____

Identify the error in each sentence as a *misplaced modifier* (MM), a *squinting modifier* (SM), a *dangling modifier* (DM), or an instance of *faulty parallelism* (FP). Then rewrite each sentence (each question, 5 points).

33. _____ Sally was grateful for a meal on her table, a roof over her head, and that family loved her.

_____

_____

34. _____ With his loud roar, the zookeeper was hesitant to feed the lion.

_____

_____

35. _____ My mother said occasionally she suffers from migraine headaches.

_____

_____

36. _____ Because of the flat tire, we nearly arrived three hours late.

_____

_____

37. _____ Knowing what to do is one thing, but to do it is quite another.

_____

_____

LANGUAGE ARTS 1104

Unit 4: Why Study Reading?

TEACHER NOTES

MATERIALS NEEDED FOR LIFEPAC	
Required	Suggested
(None)	• *World Book Dictionary* or *American Heritage Dictionary* • King James Version (KJV) of the Bible and/or other versions as permitted **Reference materials can be in printed, online, or digital formats.*

Reading affords insight into the ideas of people who lived years ago; in this way, reading differs abruptly from speaking and writing, two other means of communication. This LIFEPAC presents commonly encountered Greek and Latin prefixes and roots as a means of enlarging the students' vocabularies. Additionally, context clues, pronunciation guides, and textbook arrangement are included as further aids for improved reading skills.

EXTENDED WRITING ASSIGNMENT

Activity 4.22. For basic grading guidelines refer to the Language Arts 1101 section of the Teacher's Guide under "Extended Writing Assignment." For this assignment check the 2- to 2½-page paper for the logical development of the student's outline. The grading should take into consideration the accumulation of skills presented thus far in the LIFEPAC series.

ADDITIONAL LEARNING ACTIVITIES

Section 1: Using Prefixes and Roots

1. Let students work in small groups with a Scrabble set (students should supply or make their own). They will quickly see how the roots and prefixes from this LIFEPAC have helped increase their vocabularies.

2. Ask students to keep their flashcards handy, adding new words, roots, and prefixes as is appropriate. College-preparatory students will find a strong vocabulary will be an asset in their SAT, ACT, or GRE scores for college entrance.

Section 2: Finding Word Meanings and Pronunciation

1. Students will need their dictionaries, paper, and pencil. Read a list of ten words taken from the LIFEPAC and incorporating Greek and Latin elements. Have students look up the definitions if they have trouble with meanings of the words.

2. Students may work in small groups or independently with a literature anthology. Have students find examples of the different types of context clues (mood and atmosphere, personal experience, summary, direct explanation).

3. Students may collect examples of context clues from their outside reading. Have students keep track of the sources as a courtesy to their readers (and to their teacher).

Section 3: Finding the Main Idea

1. Students need paper and pencil. Direct students to write a paragraph with the topic sentence as the first sentence, then a paragraph where the topic sentence is the last sentence. Give students several topics from which to choose: either Biblical or class-related.

2. Have students pair up. Using the previously written paragraphs, have the partners read the material, underlining the topic sentences. The rest of the paragraph should derive from or lead to the topic sentence. Students should look for clarity and logic in the paragraphs.

3. Ask students to find an example (perhaps within a newspaper or magazine essay or editorial) of three types of paragraph constructions:

   a. topic sentence as introductory sentence followed by explanatory material,
   b. topic sentence as conclusive sentence preceded by explanatory material, and
   c. topic sentence midway through the paragraph which may be a comparison-contrast paragraph (this selection will be the most difficult for students to find, and all of the students may not be successful in locating an example).

4. Have students listen to friends and the media for variations of pronunciations. Students may record their findings over a two-week period. They should be advised to consult a dictionary to find the approved pronunciation, keeping in mind that people are often "judged" by their language, word choice, and pronunciation. Advise the students that they certainly may keep dialectical pronunciations, but that it may be helpful to the students to know (and be able to use) the pronunciations generally accepted and used by the majority of well educated English speakers.

Section 4: Analyzing a Textbook

1. With any LIFEPAC or textbook (history, Language Arts, geography, social studies, economics, or science all work well), have students outline the text as suggested in this section. A more detailed outline of a particular chapter would help demonstrate organization as well as a study skill.

2. Have each student bring several textbooks (preferably from the library and from older or younger students in order to ensure a variety of books). Students may then work in small groups of four or five, analyzing the various books and thereby proving the arrangement shown in the LIFEPAC. If any books do show a deviation, discuss the reasons for the difference with the entire class after the session has been completed. Consider the purposes of the text and the audience.

3. Have students outline a chapter from one of their LIFEPACs or textbooks. Arrangements might be made with a cooperating teacher so the assignment might have double benefits for the students.

Bible Memory Verses

Section 1
1 Timothy 4:13—give attendance to reading

Section 2
2 Corinthians 15:33—evil communications corrupt

Section 3
Galatians 6:6—communication of the Christian

Administer the LIFEPAC Test.

The test is to be administered in one session. Give no help except with directions.
Evaluate the tests and review areas where the students have done poorly.
Review the pages and activities that stress the concepts tested.
If necessary, administer the Alternate LIFEPAC Test.

ANSWER KEY

SECTION 1

1.1 preposition

1.2 Teacher check

1.3 Examples:
a. sympathy
b. antislavery
c. polyester
d. example
e. extra
f. hyperventilate
g. epidermis
h. hypodermic
i. monofilament
j. entrance
k. empathy
l. euphemism
m. catatonic
n. metaphor
o. paraprofessional
p. amphibian

1.4 a. a-   b. not
1.5 a. apo-   b. away from
1.6 a. an-   b. against, away from
1.7 a. ec-   b. out
1.8 a. ex-   b. out from
1.9 a. exo-   b. out from
1.10 a. epi-   b. upon
1.11 a. em-   b. within
1.12 a. endo-   b. within
1.13 a. pro-   b. before
1.14 a. cata-   b. down from
1.15 a. anti-   b. against
1.16 a. hyper-   b. above, over
1.17 a. hypo-   b. under
1.18 a. mono-   b. one
1.19 a. poly-   b. many
1.20 a. syl-   b. with
1.21 a. sym-   b. together
1.22 a. syn-   b. together
1.23 a. eu-   b. good
1.24 a. pan-   b. all

1.25 Teacher check

1.26 Examples:
a. permit
b. retain
c. transportation
d. benefit
e. cooperate
f. magnificent
g. contradict
h. dismiss
i. maladjusted
j. abnormal
k. senile
l. postscript
m. subway
n. ultrasonic
o. unnecessary
p. circumnavigate
q. diverse
r. adhere
s. permission
t. inverse
u. communicate
v. revert
w. unsafe
x. benediction
y. neophyte
z. miniscule
aa. semicircle

1.27
a. around
b. beyond, outside of
c. not
d. between
e. into
f. through

1.28 a. ab-   b. away, apart from, two
1.29 a. ad-   b. toward, to
1.30 a. ante-   b. before, forward
1.31 a. bene-   b. good
1.32 a. circum-   b. around
1.33 a. co-   b. with, together
1.34 a. com-   b. with, together
1.35 a. con-   b. with, together
1.36 a. contra-   b. opposite, against
1.37 a. dia-   b. through
1.38 a. di-   b. away, apart from
1.39 a. dis-   b. opposite, against
1.40 a. ef-   b. out of, away
1.41 a. e-   b. out of, away
1.42 a. e-   b. out of, away
1.43 a. eu-   b. good
1.44 a. ex-   b. out of, away
1.45 a. extra-   b. beyond, outside of

1.46	a. hyper-	b. over, above, beyond	
1.47	a. in-	b. not	
1.48	a. in-	b. into, not	
1.49	a. ir-	b. not	
1.50	a. magn-	b. great	
1.51	a. mal-	b. bad	
1.52	a. meta-	b. across	
1.53	a. mini-	b. small	
1.54	a. per-	b. through	
1.55	a. post-	b. after	
1.56	a. pre-	b. before, forward	
1.57	a. pro-	b. before, forward	
1.58	a. re-	b. back again	
1.59	a. semi-	b. half	
1.60	a. sub-	b. under	
1.61	a. super-	b. above	
1.62	a. sym-	b. together	

1.63 Examples:
a. political
b. democracy
c. aristocrat
d. patriarch
e. anthropology
f. archbishop
g. policy
h. patriot
i. archenemy
j. geography

1.64 Examples:
a. metric
b. microwave
c. photograph
d. telescope
e. thermometer
f. astronomer
g. isosceles
h. isometrics
i. helium
j. heliocentric
k. hemisphere
l. hydroelectric
m. hydrogen
n. macrocosm
o. photosynthesis
p. dynamite
q. dynamic
r. microscope
s. thermal
t. telephoto

1.65 Examples:
a. psychology
b. biology
c. cardiac

d. pneumonia
e. protoplasm
f. hemoglobin
g. skeleton
h. cardiogram
i. psychopath
j. genetic
k. arachnid
l. biopsy
m. pathology
n. thorax
o. skeletal
p. hemophilia
q. prototype
r. pseudonym
s. pneumatic
t. generate

1.66 Examples:
a. orthodox
b. theology
c. bibliography
d. ecclesiastical
e. sophist
f. martyr

1.67 Examples:
a. automatic
b. cosmic
c. cryptic
d. phonograph
e. heterogeneous
f. homogenized
g. megaphone
h. astronomy
i. petrified
j. philology
k. claustrophobia
l. philosophy
m. lithograph
n. pseudonym
o. nomenclature
p. graphics
q. microcosm
r. autograph
s. sophomore
t. megalith

1.68 Teacher check

1.69 Examples:
a. dictator
b. domestic
c. judicial
d. migrate
e. statue
f. jurisprudence

g. justice
h. static
i. dominion
j. migrant

1.70 Examples:
a. aquatic
b. science
c. terrace
d. luxurious
e. cordial
f. nuclear
g. reverse
h. converse

1.71 Examples:
a. canticle
b. incarnation
c. credential
d. crucifix
e. deity
f. fidelity
g. sanctify
h. scribble
i. script

1.72 Teacher check
1.73 e
1.74 g
1.75 n
1.76 i
1.77 d
1.78 j
1.79 b
1.80 h
1.81 m
1.82 a
1.83 k
1.84 f
1.85 Teacher check

SELF TEST 1

1.01 Either order:
a. Latin
b. Greek

1.02 Any order:
a. commerce
b. law
c. government
d. military
e. religion
f. science

1.03 Any order:
a. history
b. physical science
c. math
d. religion

1.04 b
1.05 d
1.06 a
1.07 c
1.08 d
1.09 c
1.010 a
1.011 h
1.012 c
1.013 f
1.014 l
1.015 j
1.016 d
1.017 e
1.018 g
1.019 i
1.020 k

SECTION 2

2.1 words that rhyme at the end of a line

2.2 rhyme line end device (implied) words

2.3 Example: A micrometer, or a c-shaped measuring device, was used to determine the precise thickness of the rod.

2.4 Example:
Man's spiritually deprived state—that is his separation from God—is the main source of man's social and spiritual disharmony.

2.5 facts; fiction

2.6 things known or believed to be true; the product of man's imagination.

2.7 Example:
All religions have ethical and metaphysical beliefs. We know that ethical beliefs deal with correctness of living—doing that which is right. Metaphysical beliefs however, deal with the nature of reality—that which in essence is real.

2.8 <u>ethical</u>; <u>correctness of living</u>
<u>metaphysical</u>; <u>nature of reality</u>

2.9 sad

2.10 dreadful, deadly, cruel cold death, unhappy fate, weeping eyes

2.11 Example:
Besides loving God through obeying his commandments, the Christian is to extend to his neighbor acts of love, such as forgiveness, patience, kindness, a helping hand, etc.

2.12 republicans; imperialists

2.13 Example: opposing forces

2.14 destructive to both sides

2.15 The context clues are incomplete and offer no help. The dictionary is essential.

2.16 band played; fiddlers tuned; broken sounds; murmur of voices; loud blare

2.17 mixture, conglomeration

2.18 spread itself whisperingly; arose; a buzz, or murmur; surprise; terror; horror; disgust

2.19 disapproval, rejection

2.20 Example:
Many of the Mosiac Laws given to the O.T. Hebrews have passed into disuse; however, God did not intend for his principles of life to be blatantly disregarded or totally ignored as if they were a collection of useless relics from a bygone civilization.

2.21 The vacation had a beneficial, or healthy, effect upon him.

2.22 healthy, good

2.23 compared to

2.24 equally

2.25 Example: unyielding

2.26 unmoving, unyielding

2.27 contrasted

2.28 even though ... he himself

2.29 Even though ... supporter

2.30 supporter

2.31 Example: Even though the president was somewhat agreeable to the general idea, he was adamant on rejecting the specifics of the proposal.

2.32 other ways amusing

2.33 amusing

2.34 Example: Our Lord wishes us to be steadfast and complete in our faith, avoiding transient, incomplete, changing, or anything lacking genuine qualities.

2.35 Examples:
a. The clue is an obvious one, such as an explanation.
b. The clue snaps the meaning of the whole passage.
c. The general meaning only of the word meets your purposes.

2.36 Examples:
a. When direct explanation of a word can be given.
b. When restatement by use of synonyms clarifies the word.
c. When personal experience clarifies the word.
d. When a summary clue can give meaning.
e. When words in a series can clarify

2.37 kav' əl

2.38 kə me' le ən

2.39 a. ad' vər tiz' mənt or
b. ad ver' tis mənt

2.40 thirty

2.41 short

2.42 seven

2.43 Any order: ˉ · ¨ ˆ ə Y œ

SELF TEST 2

2.01 Either order:
    a. prefixes
    b. suffixes or roots
2.02 Greeks
2.03 Any two; either order:
    a. law
    b. government
    or military, medicine, science, religion
2.04 a. fear
2.05 c. water
2.06 b. false
2.07 Example:
    expand vocabulary and comprehension for better grades in all subjects.
2.08 when a context clue supplies the word meaning and there is no need for further exact definition
2.09 usually respelled immediately following the entry, within parentheses, with an accent mark
2.010 a. direct explanation
    b. scornful
    c. scornful
2.011 a. restatement or synonyms
    b. salt, pepper, ketchup, mustard, mayonnaise
    c. foods used to add taste to the main course
2.012 a. personal experience
    b. winced, scratchy, smash, screech, poorly-played
    c. noise
2.013 a. mood, tone
    b. exaggerated
    c. amphibious animal
    d. flood

SECTION 3

3.1 obstacles; between; colonists; Dream
3.2 a. first; Spain; France; occupied; lands beyond; Appalachian
    b. the west
3.3 a. English; failed to share; vision
    b. The English were unsympathetic.
3.4 Franklin sought office.
3.5 held local elected or appointed positions: postmaster, justice of the peace, legislative clerk
3.6 wrote political tracts before French and Indian War
3.7 represented Pennsylvania in England beginning 1757
3.8 until 1775
3.9 represented other colonies
3.10 until general spokesman for all
3.11 in effect, American Ambassador
3.12 a. Franklin sought public office
    b. became justice of peace, postmaster, legislative clerk
    c. wrote political tracts before French and Indian War
    d. 1757—represented Pennsylvania in England
    e. until 1775
    f. represented other colonies
    g. until general spokesman for all
    h. in effect, American Ambassador
    i. Since before the French and Indian War, Franklin's public service included writing, serving in local appointive and elective offices, representing the colony of Pennsylvania, and finally the combined colonies in England.
3.13 Franklin served his fellow colonists from before the French and Indian War by writing political tracts, serving in local office, representing Pennsylvania in England and finally acting as a representative of the American colonies.

3.14 Underlined words:
final phase, Franklin's elected, Second Continental Congress, served on committee, drafted Declaration of Independence 1776, appointed commissioner, seek assistance, France, secured support, France and Spain, helped negotiate Treaty of Paris, England recognized American Independence, Served as delegate, Constitutional Convention

Circled words:
final, Franklin's Second Continental Congress, served, committee, drafted, Declaration of Independence, secured, support, France, Spain, helped negotiate, Treaty of Paris, serve, Constitutional Convention

a. final phase, Franklin's
b. elected Second Continental Congress, served on committee, drafted Declaration of Independence.
c. 1776, appointed commissioner, seek assistance, France
d. secured support, France and Spain, helped negotiate Treaty of Paris, England recognized American Independence
e. Served as delegate, Constitutional Convention
f. Franklin ended his career by serving in the Second Continental Congress, serving on the committee to draft the Declaration of Independence, securing support from France and Spain, helping to negotiate the Treaty of Paris, and by serving on the Constitutional Convention.

SELF TEST 3

3.01 true
3.02 false
3.03 true
3.04 true
3.05 false
3.06 false
3.07 false
3.08 false
3.09 Any five; any order:
a. direct explanation or variation
b. restatement or synonym
c. mood/tone
d. personal experience
e . summary
or comparison/contrast
words in a series
3.010 1, 2
3.011 a. Poe, inventor, detective story, ratiocinative tale
b. effect, perplex, reader, whet desire, elucidation
c. device, baffled friend, tells story
d. reader shares narrator's puzzlement
e. second device, tale's end detective discloses solution and elucidates
f. "Purloined Letter" uses both devices.
3.012 Poe, invents, ratiocinative taledevices, baffled friend, detective discloses solution
3.013 Poe invented the ratiocinative tale using two devices: the baffled friend and the detective who explains the mystery to him at the tale's end.
3.014 e—out of
3.015 luc—light
3.016 dis—down from, away from
3.017 context clue of explanation
3.018 detective story
3.019 restatement (disclose—step-by-step)
3.020 explain

SECTION 4

4.1	HISTORY OF A FREE PEOPLE
4.2	print size, all capitals
4.3	Any order:

    a. THE AMERICAN EXPERIMENT
    b. LAUNCHING THE REPUBLIC
    c. A FREE COUNTRY IN A NEW WORLD
    d. THE NATION AND THE SECTIONS
    e. DIVISION AND REUNION
    f. NEW HORIZONS
    g. CRUSADE AND DISILLUSION
    h. AN AGE OF ANXIETY
    i. THE ROOSEVELT YEARS
    j. THE EMERGENCE OF MODERN AMERICA
    k. THE COLD WAR

4.4 print size, all capitals
4.5 Any order:
    a. CRASH
    b. THE FIRST WORLD WAR
    c. THE HERITAGE OF THE COLONIAL PERIOD

4.6 Any order:
    a. Wilson's Foreign Policy—Outbreak of War in Europe
    b. Neutrality—America Enters the War
    c. The War Abroad—The Home Front—Wilson's Peace Program
    d. Aftermath of the War

4.7 print size
4.8 title
4.9 b. units
4.10 c. chapters
4.11 d. chapter sub-divisions
4.12 THE HERITAGE OF THE COLONIAL PERIOD
4.13 the title of 4.12 appears at the first level of subordination
4.14 a chapter heading
4.15 Any order:
    a. ENGLISH COLONIAL GOVERNMENT
    b. THE FRENCH COLONIES
    c. COLONIAL SOCIETY
    d. BENJAMIN FRANKLIN, PRINTER
    e. MAKING A LIVING IN THE ENGLISH COLONIES
    f. THE SPANISH COLONIES
    g. THE AGE OF DISCOVERY
    h. THE FOUNDING OF THE ENGLISH COLONIES

4.16 print size and style
4.17 Any order:
    a. Schools and Colleges
    b. Religion
    c. Effects of the Frontier
    d. Widespread Prosperity
    e. Arts and Architecture
    f. The Enlightenment
    g. Science
    h. Crêvecœur on American Life
    i. English Treatment of Indians

4.18 print size and style
4.19 chapter subsections and paragraph headings
4.20
    a. the sentence beginning with "The Variety of Religious beliefs ... "
    b. the sentence beginning with "Although many people ... "

4.21 The title represents the whole of the text; the units, the major segments of the whole idea; the chapters, the major segments of the unit idea, the subsections, the major segments of the chapter idea; the paragraph heading, the major points in a subsection; and the topic sentence, the major idea in a paragraph.

4.22 Teacher check
4.23
    a. title
    b. units
    c. chapter
    d. chapter sub-divisions or paragraph heading
    e. topic sentences
    f. text words

SELF TEST 4

4.01 l
4.02 h
4.03 e
4.04 j
4.05 a
4.06 i
4.07 c
4.08 g
4.09 d
4.010 f
4.011 chat
4.012 chau
4.013 cer
4.014 me
4.015 Examples; any order:
a. explanation
b. restatement or synonym
c. personal experience
d. summary
e. word series
or mood or atmosphere
4.016 Any order:
a. title
b. units
c. chapter
d. chapter sub-divisions or paragraph headings
e. topic sentences
f. text words
4.017 easier to identify meanings of unfamiliar words, increase reading vocabulary, better grades in schoolwork, higher scores possible on standardized tests, and so forth.
4.018 to check spelling, pronunciation, or definition of a word
4.019 title
4.020 Either order:
a. arrangement
b. print size
4.021 Greek
4.022 before
4.023 accent mark
4.024 e
4.025 a
4.026 d
4.027 b
4.028 c

4.029 marks placed over parts of words to indicate pronunciation
4.030 found out by reasoning
4.031 unstressed vowel sound represented by the symbol ə
4.032 the attitude of an author as recreated by the book
4.033 words before and after the word in a sentence that influences or explains the meaning of the word

LIFEPAC TEST

1.	false	**38.**	accent mark
2.	false	**39.**	schwa
3.	false	**40.**	diacritical marks
4.	true	**41.**	bē
5.	false	**42.**	fäther
6.	true	**43.**	no mark
7.	true	**44.**	Examples; any order:

1. false
2. false
3. false
4. true
5. false
6. true
7. true
8. true
9. false
10. true
11. b. love
12. c. knowledge
13. j. belief
14. s. lead
15. o. break
16. c. knowledge
17. d. man
18. w. color
19. t. earth
20. m. blood
21. p. water
22. g. small
23. i. before
24. v. opposite *or*
k. against
25. q. great
26. g. small
27. i. before *and/or*
r. in front of
28. x. old
29. h. bath
30. k. against
31. l. out from
32. u. under
33. n. all
34. r. in front of *and/or*
i. before
35. a. laziness
b. the "doing of nothing" by "direct explanation"
36. a. practical or useful rather than fun-oriented or unproductive
b. the opposite of "entertain" by "synonym restatement"
37. a. slavery
b. the clues are "reduced, under harness," and "curb, drudgery" or "mood or atmosphere"

38. accent mark
39. schwa
40. diacritical marks
41. bē
42. fäther
43. no mark
44. Examples; any order:
a. title
b. units
c. chapters
d. chapter sub-division or paragraph headings
e. topic sentence or paragraphs
f. text words

ALTERNATE LIFEPAC TEST

1.	e
2.	g
3.	b
4.	i
5.	h
6.	c
7.	a
8.	j
9.	d
10.	f
11.	true
12.	false
13.	true
14.	false
15.	false
16.	true
17.	true
18.	true
19.	true
20.	true
21.	synonyms
22.	accent mark
23.	summary
24.	dictionary
25.	root

LANGUAGE ARTS 1104

ALTERNATE LIFEPAC TEST

NAME _____

DATE _____

SCORE _____

Match these items (each answer, 4 points).

1. _____ amphi-

2. _____ hypo-

3. _____ anti-

4. _____ pan-

5. _____ cogn-

6. _____ amor-

7. _____ cred-

8. _____ magn-

9. _____ ex-

10. _____ anthropo-

a. belief

b. against

c. love

d. out from

e. both

f. man

g. under

h. knowledge

i. forward

j. great

k. all

Answer *true* **or** *false* (each answer, 4 points).

11. _____ Personal experience can be a context clue.

12. _____ A root is added to the end of a word.

13. _____ The most important sentence in a paragraph is usually the first one.

14. _____ Many English words are formed from Greek and Latin prefixes added to the end of a word.

15. _____ An unfamiliar word should always be looked up in a dictionary.

16. _____ The schwa indicates the indeterminate vowel sound.

17. _____ A topic sentence will usually be found as either the first sentence, or occasionally as the last sentence, of a paragraph.

18. _____ Diacritical marks are placed above vowels and consonants to aid pronunciation.

19. _____ Type size in a textbook may be used to indicate the relative importance of ideas.

20. _____ Greek and Latin prefixes and roots may be encountered in school subjects like mathematics, science, English, chemistry, and religion.

Complete these statements (each answer, 4 points).

21. _Roget's Thesaurus_ is a dictionary of _____ and antonyms which can be helpful in deciphering context clues.

22. The pronunciation aid that determines the stress placed upon a syllable is the

    _____ .

23. The _____ context clue occurs when a single word seems to include or to describe a whole situation.

24. The only safe guide for determining the proper pronunciation of a word is the

    _____ .

25. The _____ of a word carries the burden of its meaning; the prefix or suffix alters that meaning.

LANGUAGE ARTS 1105

Unit 5: Poetry

TEACHER NOTES

MATERIALS NEEDED FOR LIFEPAC	
Required	Suggested
(None)	• any American poetry anthology or American literature anthology • *World Book Dictionary* or *American Heritage Dictionary* • King James Version (KJV) of the Bible and/or other versions as permitted • Ellman, Richard and Robert O'Clair (eds.). *The Norton Anthology of Modern Poetry*. New York: W.W. Norton and Company, Inc., Latest Edition. (or any other good American literature anthology) **Reference materials can be in printed, online, or digital formats.*

In this LIFEPAC, the student will examine the art of poetry in three ways: (1) the analysis of poetic form and measurement, (2) the definition of universal meanings, and (3) the examination of imagery and connotation in poetic language. Each of these three methods of examination is illustrated within the LIFEPAC by specific poems, some quoted in part and others reproduced in full text. The activities include some attempt at poetic writing by the students themselves; guidelines for these attempts are included in the instructions for individual activities.

EXTENDED WRITING ASSIGNMENT

No long paper has been assigned in the LIFEPAC itself, but one will be included in the Additional Learning Activities for the last Independent Project in this Teacher's Guide.

ADDITIONAL LEARNING ACTIVITIES

Section 1: Measurement and Form

1. Of the five styles of poetry discussed—lyric, narrative, sonnet, blank verse, and free verse—choose one example of each from an anthology and read them aloud in class, being careful to point out the differences in each style.

2. First divide the class into groups of four or five. Have each group choose one poem by either Poe or Longfellow. Have students pick out the musical devices and kinds of rhyme found in each poem.

3. Seven authors are used in the illustrative examples in this section. Have students choose any poem not in this LIFEPAC by any one of the seven poets. Scan that particular poem and mark the proper meter and rhyme scheme the poet has chosen. Each student could report their findings to the class.

Section 2: Universality

1. America has long been considered the hope of much of the free world, and her poets have used this theme of hope often in their work. Locate some of the early patriotic poems of poets like Longfellow, Lowell, Emerson, or Holmes and share them with the class. Suggestions: Longfellow's "The Building of a Ship," Holmes's "God Save the Flag," or Emerson's "Concord Hymn."

2. Organize class discussions concerning the three universal experiences dealt with by poetry. If possible, let the students choose poems that they think illustrate any one of these three experiences and share their choices with the rest of the group.

3. Have students take the poem picked in the group discussion and write a brief paper (250 words or less) explaining and defending the choice made in the preceding activity.

Section 3: Imagery and Connotation

1. Figures of speech are the tools of imagery in poetry. To ensure that the students can distinguish between the various kinds of figurative language (simile, metaphor, personification), go over several poems in class and point out the different kinds of images used in each. Suggestion: Any Robert Frost poem is usually rich in all these figures of speech.

2. Divide the class into small groups of two or three. Have each group compose a list of original similes, metaphors, and personifications (three or four of each) and then share them with the rest of the class.

3. Since no lengthy writing assignment was given in the LIFEPAC, the last project will be a short poetry analysis. Each student should choose one poem by any American author and write a short paper (about 250 words) about that poem. The student may deal with any one of the three areas covered in this LIFEPAC—measurement and form, universal meaning, or imagery and connotation—in this paper, but make certain that the paper is limited to only one of the three areas. In grading this writing assignment, refer first to the writing guidelines given in detail in the 1101 section of this Teacher's Guide. The mechanics of construction are obviously important. The first four LIFEPACs in this series took the students step by step through the writing process. Check now in this paper to see if the students are using the techniques (compound-complex sentences and appositives, for example) they have learned earlier. Examine the logical organization and presentation of the material, and remember that student originality should be considered very important.

Bible Memory Verses

Section 1
Psalm 95—example of a lyric poem

Section 2
Matthew 17:20—faith
Psalm 39:7—hope
1 Corinthians 13:13—charity (love)

Section 3
Psalm 1:1—example of a simile
Solomon 2:1—example of a metaphor
Psalm 92:7—example of personification

Administer the LIFEPAC Test.

The test is to be administered in one session. Give no help except with directions.
Evaluate the tests and review areas where the students have done poorly.
Review the pages and activities that stress the concepts tested.
If necessary, administer the Alternate LIFEPAC Test.

ANSWER KEY

SECTION 1

1.1   a. yes
        b. no
        c. yes
        d. yes
        e. no

1.2   Bý ă routé ŏbscuré ańd lońelў.

1.3   Example
        Cańrў pénniës iń yŏur póckĕt.

1.4   a. Ĭt wăs máný and máný ă yéar ago.
        b. iamb

1.5   Examples:
        a. Annabel and the narrator fell in love in a seaside town.
        b. They were so deeply in love that the angels in heaven envied the intensity of their love.
        c. The angels' jealousy was the reason that a chill wind killed Annabel and she was buried by her royal relatives.
        d. The stanza repeats the assertion that the angels killed Annabel Lee.
        e. Their love was stronger than that of older and wiser people, and neither angels nor demons can separate the soul of the two lovers.
        f. His every thought is of Annabel and at night he lies down by her side in the sepulcher by the sea.

1.6   Examples:
        a. somber, eerie, supernatural
        b. melancholy, grieving, resentful. The narrator is driven to madness and cannot see things as they are.

1.7   Teacher check

1.8   a. anapests
        b. dactyls

1.9   a. iambic
        b. masculine
        c. anapestic
        d. masculine
        e. trochaic
        f. feminine

1.10   a. meek, flock
        b. a trochee
        c. one whose

1.11   a. buḿblĕbeĕ
        b. teétĕr tottĕr

        c. a trŭe talé ŏf thĕ dayś ŏf hĭs youŭth
        d. Bĕsidé thĕ séa ăn ofd grĕy dóg

1.12   Self check

1.13   Examples:
        a. welcome
        b. sum
        c. dumb
        d. appeal
        e. conceal
        f. pinwheel
        g. fatherland
        h. underhand
        i. overhand

1.14   Examples:
        a. give
        b. five

1.15   a. a
        b. a
        c. b
        d. b
        e. a
        f. a
        g. a
        h. c
        i . c
        j. a
        k. a
        l. a
        m. d
        n. d
        o. a

1.16   *aa bba aacca aadda*

1.17   by the repetition of the line "And the tide rises, the tide falls."

1.18   Teacher check

1.19   a. strength, stretch
        b. barely, bleed, bruised
        c. round, room
        d. rage, reason

1.20   a. peck, beak
        b. tomb, room

1.21   no

1.22   no

1.23   Hint:
        Consider both the description of the chick's experience and the application of that experience to human beings.

1.24 Example:
Many people have seen the process of a chick coming out of its shell. Few people have asked, "How is this experience like something in my life?" In asking that question, the poet gives the act uncommon meaning.

1.25 Hint:
You may wish to refer to Philippians 4:13 and to Proverbs 16:32, or you may use other applicable passages with which you are familiar.

1.26
a. consonance
b. imperfect rhyme
c. imperfect rhyme
d. consonance
e. alliteration
f. consonance

1.27 Either order:
a. alliteration
b. consonance

1.28 Examples:
a. colt
b. cat
c. pest

1.29 Examples:
a. colt
b. cattle
c. kitten

1.30 Examples:
from, huddled, ugly, sudden; lake, waves, breaking, spray; fluttering, gulls; great, gray, flying, white; veering, wheeling, free

1.31 alliteration: sudden, city, sun, spray, storm; internal rhyme: lake and break

1.32 Example:
The contrast between crowded, ugly buildings and the freedom of the gull flying above the open sea.

1.33
a. whistled, echoing, rumbling
b. warble, reedy
c. a locomotive
d. a bird

1.34
a. rushing, roaring, shrill, whistle
b. Example:
   speed
c. Example:
   rumbling—the noise of the train
d. alliteration, assonance, and consonance

1.35
a. yes
b. yes
c. yes
d. yes
e. yes

1.36
a. Petrarchan
b. Shakespearean

1.37
a. Italian (corresponds to Petrarchan)
   abbaabba cde cde
b. English (corresponds to Shakespearean)
   abab cdcd efef gg

1.38 Teacher check

1.39
a. no end rhyme
b. iambic pentameter

1.40 free verse has no meter

1.41 Shakespeare

1.42 Walt Whitman

1.43 Any order:
a. fourteen lines
b. set rhyme scheme
c. iambic pentameter

1.44 Hint:
Answer should mention that narrative verse tells a story and that lyric verse has song-like qualities.

1.45 d

1.46 e

1.47 c

1.48 a

SELF TEST 1

1.01 true
1.02 true
1.03 false
1.04 false
1.05 false
1.06 onomatopoeia
1.07 iamb
1.08 a. correspondence of sound
   b. initial consonants
   c. accented on the same syllable
1.09 b
1.010 d
1.011 a
1.012 a
1.013 b
1.014 iamb
1.015 dactyl
1.016 dactyl
1.017 trochee
1.018 trochee
1.019 dactyl
1.020 anapest
1.021 trochee
1.022 iamb
1.023 trochee
1.024 mono
1.025 di
1.026 tri
1.027 tetra
1.028 penta
1.029 hexa
1.030 hepta
1.031 octa
1.032 trochaic
1.033 tetrameter
1.034 trimeter (incomplete last foot)
1.035 *abcb*
1.036 rhythm or trochee
1.037 assonance
1.038 alliteration
1.039 d
1.040 b
1.041 c
(1.042–1.043: Either order)
1.042 octave
1.043 sestet

SECTION 2

2.1 the poet (narrator)
2.2 nature
2.3 nature
2.4 Example:
One won't be alone; the tomb (earth) is beautiful.
2.5 Suppose no one cares?
2.6 Everyone else will share the same fate.
2.7 Example:
Live while you have life and when you die, don't slink resentfully to your grave but accept death peacefully.
2.8 no
2.9 Example:
resignation
2.10 A clerk in the department of records.
2.11 The type that can be obtained from birth certificates, employment records, and other documents.
2.12 Example:
The true identity of the citizen can't be obtained from public records, even if his name is on file.
2.13 Example:
The meter is not so much forced as ignored and the rhyme scheme is irregular. The poet is making the clerk look ridiculous.
2.14 Example:
As long as they keep quiet and pay their bills, they're harmless.
2.15 Example:
The poet is outraged by bureaucracies indifference.
2.16 Hint:
You may find that the poem reads very much like prose.
2.17 Hint:
What criticisms is the poet making of today's society?
2.18 Example:
I was awakened by a terrible noise. The house was burning. I cried to God to give me help and strength. Then I blessed God, realizing it was his own goods He was taking, not mine. He could justly have taken more than He took. I remember where all my precious furniture stood. Now it will never be used again. No life will go on under this roof. All is vanity. Then I chide myself for such thoughts. My trust should be in God, not the things of man. I have a house in heaven that nothing can take from me. I don't need earthly treasures; my treasure is in heaven.

2.19 no
2.20 Because Jefferson was the author of the Declaration of Independence.
2.21 Example:
MacLeish believes that people valued their freedom during Jefferson's time, giving their lives for it, but that now we talk about freedom but don't preserve it for anyone but ourselves.
2.22 Line 37—Franco's Fascist dictatorship in Spain
Line 39-40—Peron's dictatorship in Argentina
Line 43—The crushing of a Hungarian revolt by Russia
2.23 Example:
He was born in 1892. His generation was willing to fight for freedom in World War I (see lines 29–32).
2.24 Example:
At the beginning of the poem, the poet points out that Tyrants feared men of integrity who committed themselves to all of the implication of Freedom. Now (end of poem) we no longer have that moral commitment and the old world cynically ignores our pretty words which reflect no commitment.
2.25 no
Example:
If the poet were convinced that the freedom was lost forever, he would not have taken the time or effort to write the poem, or if he had, his tone would have been one of bereavement rather than criticism.
2.26 Teacher check
2.27 Hint:
Rural, family—and church-centered, farming.
2.28 line 14
2.29 the daughter
2.30 the poet (narrator)
2.31 the daughter, the mother, and the poet
2.32 Example:
It adds to the reader's empathy for the people in the poem, helping him to feel what they feel.
2.33 none

2.34 Example:
It resembles speech and is therefore appropriate for ordinary people.
2.35 Examples:
a. Who killed this man's spirit?
b. Is this what God intended man to be?
c. What are the wondrous creations of God to someone who cannot appreciate them?
d. O rulers, how will you ever repair the damage you have done?
e. How will God judge the rulers of mankind for this crime against humanity?
2.36 Example:
Line 11—reference to creation. Numerous references to God (lines 15, 34, etc.) Reference to the day of judgment in stanza five. Quotation at beginning of poem.
2.37 Examples:
a. Pity, revulsion, grief at his ignorance and insensibility.
b. Anger that they have ruined the lives of other human beings; hope that they will see what they have done before it is too late.
2.38 Any order:
meter
alliteration
assonance
consonance
2.39 Example:
The poet's skill gives his poem a formality that intensifies its seriousness.
2.40 Hint:
Details are given in the first stanza. Inference may be made from the rest of the poem.
2.41 God loved us so much that He laid down his life for us.
2.42 Essentially the theme agrees.
2.43 died, side; alone, groan, then, ten
2.44 sad, bad; then, ten; embrace, place; there, where
2.45 did, died; His, heaven; Lord, Life; die, depending, did, died
2.46 sad, good, bad; died, side; who, how, who
2.47 His, is, stripped; born, score

SELF TEST 2

2.01 false
2.02 true
2.03 false
2.04 true
2.05 true
2.06 false
2.07 true
2.08 false
2.09 false
2.010 false
2.011 false
2.012 c
2.013 g
2.014 e
2.015 a
2.016 b
2.017 h
2.018 f
2.019 i
2.020 iambic pentameter
2.021 *abba*, *abba*, *cde*, *cde*
2.022 an Italian sonnet
2.023 b
2.024 b
2.025 b
2.026 love for other human beings based on common humanity.
2.027 love focused upon God or upon some cause higher than self or other human beings.
2.028 expectation of fulfillment of a desire.
2.029 a conviction or belief held without need for proof.
2.030 the pattern of rhymes in a stanza or poem
2.031 five metrical feet to a line
2.032 repeated initial consonant sounds
2.033 a substitute foot consisting of the accented syllables.

SECTION 3

3.1 lines 18–20—Trailing them leaves on the ground like girls on hands and knees that then—their hair before them … sun."
3.2 Life is like a pathless wood.
3.3 Example:
Life is confusing because a person can go in many directions, none of them easy.
3.4 no
3.5 a. daisy
b. pie
c. lark
d. pig
3.6 Examples:
a. Fresh as newly-baked bread
b. as easy as blinking my eye
c. Happy as a child on Christmas
d. Working like an ant at a picnic
3.7 a. cracks and crazes their enamel
b. shed crystal shells
c. heaps of broken glass
3.8 a. cracks and crazes this bark like enamel
b. shed drips of ice like crystal shells
c. piles of ice like heaps of broken glass
3.9 a. The sea "calls" (line 7)
b. little waves with their soft, white hands (line 8)
3.10 (line 1) sea awoke from sleep
3.11 Teacher check

SELF TEST 3

3.01   a. iamb
         b. trochee
3.02   a. faith
         b. hope
         c. love
3.03   lyric
3.04   simile
3.05   metaphor
3.06   personification
3.07   denotative
3.08   connotations
3.09   false
3.010 false
3.011 true
3.012 true
3.013 true
3.014 false
3.015 true
3.016 true
3.017 e
3.018 g
3.019 f
3.020 d
3.021 a
3.022 b
3.023 h
3.024 c
3.025 i
3.026 a
3.027 c
3.028 a
3.029 a
3.030 b
3.031 b
3.032 a. simile
         b. a comparison using *like* or *as*
         c. metaphor
         d. an implied comparison (something is
            called something else)
         e. personification
         f. something nonhuman is given human
            characteristics

LIFEPAC TEST

1. false
2. false
3. false
4. false
5. true
6. false
7. true
8. false
9. true
10. false
11. true
12. false
13. false
14. b
15. c
16. c
17. b
18. d
19. e
20. g
21. a
22. f
23. c
24. b
25. e
26. b
27. h
28. g
29. f
30. c
31. d
32. a
33. c
34. consonance
35. onomatopoeia
36. epic
37. connotation

ALTERNATE LIFEPAC TEST

1. true
2. true
3. false
4. false
5. true
6. false
7. false
8. true
9. true
10. false
11. b
12. a
13. c
14. d
15. b
16. b
17. c
18. a
19. d
20. a
21. d
22. k
23. h
24. a
25. b
26. j
27. i
28. c
29. e
30. f
31. rhyme scheme
32. Any order:
   a. faith
   b. hope
   c. love
33. connotations
34. brotherly love
35. metrical sets

LANGUAGE ARTS 1105

ALTERNATE LIFEPAC TEST

NAME _____

DATE _____

SCORE _____

81 / 101

Answer *true* **or** *false* (each answer, 2 points).

1. _____ Feminine and masculine endings are determined by the stressed or unstressed syllables at the end of a line of poetry.

2. _____ The most common meter in English poetry is iambic pentameter.

3. _____ Only one kind of rhyme is used in English poetry.

4. _____ A series of repeated initial consonant sounds is called onomatopoeia.

5. _____ Lyric poetry is based on a song-like quality.

6. _____ The sonnet is a poetic form popular with many American poets.

7. _____ Meter and rhyme schemes are determined by a method called alliteration.

8. _____ William Cullen Bryant wrote "Thanatopsis" about man's faith in nature.

9. _____ Archibald MacLeish's poem "Brave New World" expresses the universal experience of hope.

10. _____ Eye rhyme refers to words that both sound alike and look alike.

Write the correct letter on each line (each answer, 3 points).

11. A comparison in which the words *as* or *like* are used is the _____ .
    a. metaphor   b. simile   c. dactyl   d. personification

12. The kind of sonnet usually adapted by American poets is the _____ .
    a. Italian   b. masculine   c. anapestic   d. lyric

13. A poet endowing animals, objects, or abstract ideas with human characteristics is using the figure of speech called _____ .
    a. exaggeration   b. alliteration   c. personification   d. simile

14. One type of narrative poetry written in stanzas is the _____ .
    a. song   b. sonnet   c. lyric   d. ballad

15. A kind of figurative language that draws a sharper comparison than a simile is a(n) _____ .
    a. hyperbole   b. metaphor   c. connotation   d. assonance

16. Walt Whitman's "Song of Myself" is an illustration of _____ .
    a. hope   b. man-centered faith
    c. love   d. nature-centered faith

17. The most common metrical foot in English poetry is the _____ .
    a. trochee   b. anapest   c. iamb   d. dactyl

18. The most familiar musical effect in poetry is _____ .
    a. rhyme   b. song   c. assonance   d. alliteration

19. The Psalms of David are a well-known Biblical example of the universal human experience of _____ .
    a. faith in nature   b. faith in man   c. faith in self   d. faith in God

20. More poetry has been written about _____ than any other human experience.
    a. love   b. faith   c. hope   d. nature

Match these items (each answer, 3 points).

21. _____ Edgar Allen Poe

22. _____ octave

23. _____ Walt Whitman

24. _____ blank verse

25. _____ "Thanatopsis"

26. _____ "The Courtin'"

27. _____ image

28. _____ alliteration

29. _____ trochee

30. _____ Robert Frost

a. unrhymed iambic pentameter

b. an example of nature-centered faith

c. a series of repeated consonant sounds

d. "Annabel Lee"

e. a two-syllable foot that is the direct reverse of an iamb

f. "Birches"

g. "The Harbour"

h. pioneer of free verse

i. a word picture

j. a poetic example of romantic love

k. the section of a sonnet that sets the theme

Complete these statements (each answer, 3 points).

31. A poet who follows a particular pattern in his rhyming is said to use a(n) _____ _____ .

32. The three universal experiences poets write about are a. _____ , b. _____ , and c. _____ .

33. Suggested meanings of words that go beyond literal dictionary definitions are _____ .

34. Whitman's Civil War poem "Come Up From the Fields Father" is an illustration of _____ .

35. A planned group of syllables in specific patterns that tie together metrical feet are _____ .

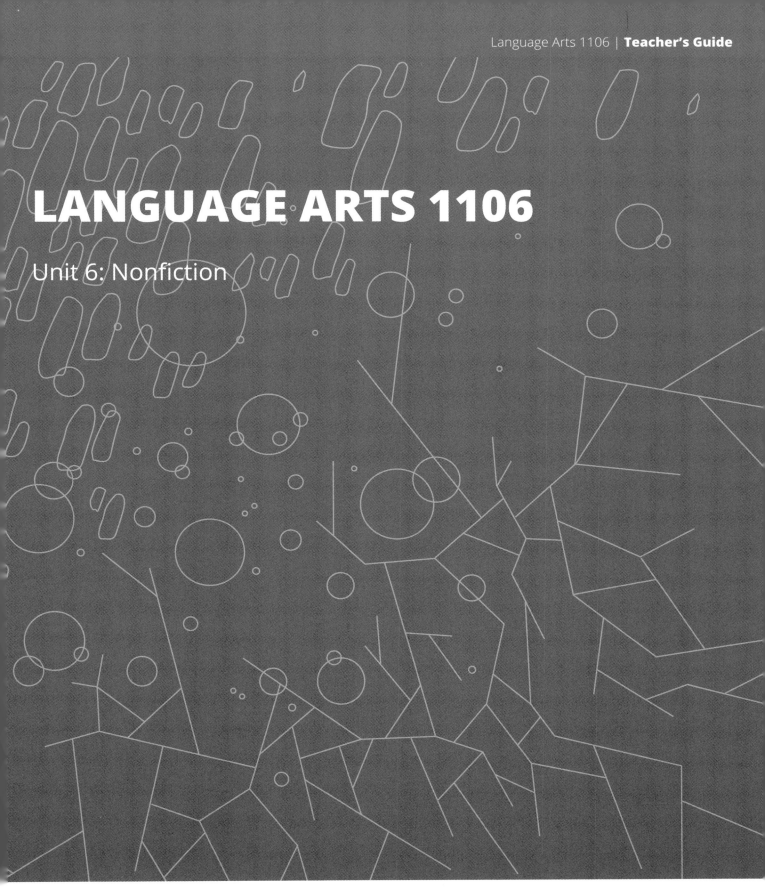

LANGUAGE ARTS 1106

Unit 6: Nonfiction

TEACHER NOTES

MATERIALS NEEDED FOR LIFEPAC	
Required	Suggested
(None)	• *World Book Dictionary* or *American Heritage Dictionary* • King James Version (KJV) of the Bible and/or other versions as permitted • a loose-leaf notebook or tablet to use as a journal • a current local newspaper • Jefferson, Thomas. "The Declaration of Independence." • Hamilton, Alexander and James Madison. *The Federalist Papers* **Reference materials can be in printed, online, or digital formats.*

In this LIFEPAC, the student will examine the elements, types, topics, and composition of nonfiction. This detailed examination will include the definition, form, and characteristics of this kind of literature as well as a series of carefully chosen prose selections for student reading. An explanation of the art of composing nonfiction and a discussion of guidelines for choosing possible topics for such composition conclude this study.

EXTENDED WRITING ASSIGNMENT

No long paper is assigned in this LIFEPAC, but three shorter assignments involving the three types of expository composition are assigned. Describing the grading of these compositions in this section is not necessary because that process has been described in detail for each paper in the preceding teacher checklist.

ADDITIONAL LEARNING ACTIVITIES

Section 1: Elements of Nonfiction

1. Devote a class period to a discussion of the importance of nonfiction in today's society. Try to include in your discussion the function of online media, newspapers, news reports, magazines, and nonfiction books on today's thinking.

2. Divide the students into three groups. Let each group choose one of the following patterns of expository prose: argumentative, analytical, or illustrative. Then have each group bring to class one nonfiction article, essay, editorial, or sermon that illustrates their choice. (Possible sources are the Internet, newspapers, magazines, encyclopedias, etc.)

3. Each student should choose a brief selection of descriptive prose (one in LIFEPAC 1106 will do) and go through it to pick out the figurative language used by the author. The student should then make a list of those images, dividing them into similes, metaphors, personifications, and hyperboles, and share those lists with the rest of the class.

Section 2: Types of Nonfiction

1. Choose one of the famous and more important diaries or journals (Dr. Samuel Johnson's, for example) and read aloud brief selections from it to the class.

2. Divide the class into groups of four or five. Have each group take one newspaper or magazine editorial and discuss the analytical composition of the piece. (Example: What is the writer's viewpoint? How did the writer choose to present that opinion? Did they succeed in convincing his reader? If not, why not?)

3. Each student should choose one work of nonfiction (a short biography, a collection of essays, a diary, or a brief history) and read it outside of class. Written book reports are unnecessary but possibly a few oral reports might be presented.

Section 3: Topics and Composition in Nonfiction

1. Share some modern nonfiction with the class. Possibly certain newspaper or online columnists who use humor as a basis of their writing might be an interesting change of pace for the students.

2. Ideas are one of the most important subjects of nonfiction. Let the class examine together one piece of American philosophy such as Emerson's "Commodity," Crèvecœur's thoughts on America in letters from an American Farmer, or Jonathan Edwards's study of spiritual growth in his *Personal Narrative* (all these and several other suitable selections can be found in Language Arts LIFEPAC 1106).

3. In order to review analytical, illustrative, and argumentative patterns of writing, each student should choose ten subjects for compositions, pick titles for those subjects, and then decide which particular one of the three patterns would best develop each subject. These titles and pattern choices should be listed and turned in.

Bible Memory Verses

Section 1
Psalm 45:1—the importance of writing

Section 2
Matthew 5:1–48—an example of a sermon, Christ's Sermon on the Mount
1 Corinthians—an example of Biblical letters, the letters to the Christians at Corinth

Section 3
Hebrews 13:16—the value of composition and communication

Administer the LIFEPAC Test.

The test is to be administered in one session. Give no help except with directions.
Evaluate the tests and review areas where the students have done poorly.
Review the pages and activities that stress the concepts tested.
If necessary, administer the Alternate LIFEPAC Test.

ANSWER KEY

SECTION 1

1.1   false
1.2   false
1.3   false
1.4   false
1.5   true
1.6   true
1.7   false
1.8   true
1.9   false
1.10 Examples:
    a. one
    b. five
1.11 Examples:
    a. *Newsweek*
    b. *Time*
1.12 Examples:
    a. *Reader's Digest*
    b. *New York Times*
    c. Mark Twain's *Life on the Mississippi*
1.13 Any order:
    a. clarity
    b. conciseness
    c. completeness
    d. coherence
1.14 Any order:
    a. illustrative
    b. analytical
    c. argumentative
1.15 Any order:
    a. example
    b. definition
    c. comparison or contrast
    d. supporting detail
1.16 true
1.17 true
1.18 false
1.19 false
1.20 c
1.21 b
1.22 d
1.23 e, b
1.24 a, d
1.25 f, h
1.26 j, g

1.27 Examples:
    a. "I am become <u>as</u> sounding brass, or a tinkling cymbal."
    b. "The spirit of man is the candle of the Lord ..."
    c. " ... neither cast your pearls before swine ..."
    d. "Charity suffereth long, and is kind; charity envieth not; charity vaunteth not itself, is not puffed up ... "

SELF TEST 1

1.01	e		
1.02	i		
1.03	k		
1.04	h		
1.05	m		
1.06	l		
1.07	d		
1.08	n		
1.09	f		
1.010	a		

1.011 c. factual
1.012 c. Explains a subject by illustration
1.013 d. follows a logical pattern
1.014 a. tries to convince the reader
1.015 b. a witty, chatty approach
1.016 false
1.017 true
1.018 false
1.019 false
1.020 true
1.021 false
1.022 true
1.023 true
1.024 false
1.025 true
1.026 Any order:
    a. clarity
    b. conciseness
    c. coherence
    d. completeness
1.027 Any order:
    a. know the subject; check up on missing details of information
    b. make a logical plan or outline
    c. include all necessary facts
    d. arrange all the facts in a clear, concise, coherent pattern
    e. use an interesting opening to catch the reader's attention
    f. decide on the pattern development required for the purpose
1.028 Any order:
    a. illustrative pattern
    b. analytical pattern
    c. argumentative pattern
1.029 Either order:
    a. fiction is based on imaginative story development with plot; and so forth
    b. nonfiction is factual, actual, descriptive, covers some five major genres

1.030 Either order:
    a. wide-spread availability
    b. lack of time to read lengthy fiction
1.031 exposition
1.032 descriptive
1.033 figurative language
1.034 Any order:
    a. simile
    b. metaphor
    c. hyperbole
    d. personification
1.035 vignette
1.036 propaganda
1.037 analytical
1.038 illustrative
1.039 argumentative

SECTION 2

2.1   try or attempt
2.2   Either order:
      a.   formal
      b.   informal
2.3   thoughts
2.4   Michel Montaigne
2.5   Francis Bacon
2.6   Either order:
      a.   Joseph Addison
      b.   Richard Steele
2.7   Either order:
      a.   Wordsworth
      b.   Coleridge
2.8   short, transient, not of long duration
2.9   Example:
      It might make them think seriously about their own souls.
2.10   true
2.11   false
2.12   true
2.13   true
2.14   false
2.15   true
2.16   true
2.17   Either order:
      a.   personal enjoyment
      b.   historical record for posterity
2.18   Smith's *A True Relation*
2.19   fictional or imaginative
2.20   encounter with the Native Americans
2.21   a.   logs
      Either order:
      b.   pine
      c.   cypress
2.22   Jefferson's letter to Thomas Paine
2.23   Hint:
      Set a special time each day to write. You might be interested in checking out journals kept by other famous people for ideas.
2.24   historical background
2.25   John Winthrop
2.26   an author's story about himself
2.27   Benjamin Franklin
2.28   Either order:
      a.   newspapers
      b.   magazines
2.29   anthology

2.30   Any order:
      a.   who
      b.   what
      c.   when
      d.   where
      e.   how
2.31   editorial
2.32   Any order:
      a.   political
      b.   social
      c.   economic
2.33   Example:
      political

SELF TEST 2

2.01 e
2.02 f
2.03 b
2.04 h
2.05 a
2.06 c
2.07 l
2.08 k
2.09 d
2.010 i
2.011 false
2.012 true
2.013 false
2.014 false
2.015 true
2.016 true
2.017 false
2.018 vignettes
2.019 the climax
2.020 analytical
2.021 propaganda
2.022 conciseness
2.023 coherence
2.024 dealing with fact
2.025 exposition
2.026 Either order:
    a. formal
    b. informal
2.027 b
2.028 d
2.029 b
2.030 c
2.031 a
2.032 an essay stating the opinion of a publisher or editor
2.033 short
2.034 An essay is an attempt to briefly express ideas, views, feelings, or reactions to situations in life. It may be serious or witty.
2.035 Any order:
    a. who
    b. what
    c. when
    d. where
    e. how
2.036 Any order:
    a. essay sermon
    b. diary, journal or letter
    c. biography or autobiography
    d. articles or editorial

SECTION 3

3.1 they know

3.2 spiritual

3.3 a thunderstorm

3.4 complete Christian

3.5 "a proud and self-righteous"

3.6 Teacher check

3.7 they helped the Jews by hiding them in their own home

3.8 Either order:
   a. her father died
   b. her sister died

3.9 Any order:
   a. cold
   b. little food
   c. cruel treatment
   d. forced prisoners to work

3.10 her Christian faith

3.11 visited groups to tell about her experiences and her faith

3.12 One of the Nazis who had tormented the prisoners appeared at one of her meetings. He was impressed by her faith and extended his hand. She was torn by her memories and anger.

3.13 She prayed. She asked Jesus to forgive him for her. She immediately felt Christian love and shook hands with her former enemy.

3.14 the personality of the subject

3.15 Either order:
   a. setting
   b. history

3.16 a. teacher
   b. rural hills of Kentucky

3.17 cruel

3.18 Robert E. Lee

3.19 a. Carl Sandburg
   b. Abraham Lincoln

3.20 a. ✓   b. ✓
   c.   d. ✓

3.21 Student check

3.22 d

3.23 d

3.24 a

3.25 b

3.26 c

3.27 the quality that makes something seem funny, amusing, ludicrous, or comical

3.28 It can relieve tension, giving the reader a break from serious or heavily emotional material.

3.29 Any order:
   a. entertainment
   b. a method of criticism
   c. emotional release

3.30 A literary device blending humor with criticism to attain social or political reform.

3.31 a. a form of literature written by a poet
   b. a passenger vehicle having four wheels and self-propelled by an engine
   c. an explanation in speech or writing

3.32 Example:
An automobile is a passenger vehicle having four wheels and being self-propelled by an engine. Automobiles may have two or four doors. Some models, called hatchbacks, have an extra door in the back, similar to that of a station wagon. Automobiles are available in all sizes, ranging from the sub-compact to the limousine. The red 2016 Camaro in the parking lot is my teacher's automobile.

3.33 Example:
Point-by-point:
   I. State University
      A. variety of courses available
      B. tuition
      C. reputation of school
   II. Community College
      A. variety of courses available
      B. tuition
      C. reputation of school

3.34 Point-by-point is more suitable for long, complex essays. Extended comparison or contrast is more suitable for shorter papers.

3.35 Teacher check

3.36 Teacher check

3.37 Teacher check

SELF TEST 3

3.01   h
3.02   l
3.03   j
3.04   i
3.05   f
3.06   d
3.07   e
3.08   b
3.09   a
3.010 c
3.011 Write the classification to which the word belongs; explain any ways this word differs from others in its class; give an example.
3.012 to realize the effect his writings may have because of the power of the written word to influence others for good or bad; to the public
3.013 a. positive—when it emphasizes desirable outcomes
           b. negative—when it distorts truth for evil purposes
3.014 Actual happenings and people are often more unusual, fantastic, and unreal than fictional happenings and people.
3.015 false
3.016 false
3.017 true
3.018 true
3.019 false
3.020 true
3.021 false
3.022 true
3.023 true
3.024 false
3.025 type of writing which convinces readers
3.026 not true to fact or actuality; made-up
3.027 past events or remembrances
3.028 short, delicate, compact literary composition frequently about a favorite person
3.029 personal ideas or thoughts on a subject; a judgment
3.030 type or classification of art or literature

3.031 Any order:
           a. personal experiences
           b. biography and autobiography
           c. ideas
           d. humor
3.032 Either order:
           a. Jonathan Edwards
           b. Corrie ten Boom
3.033 Either order:
           a. Carl Sandburg
           b. Robert E. Lee
3.034 4
3.035 6
3.036 1
3.037 3
3.038 2
3.039 5

LIFEPAC TEST

1. e
2. g
3. m
4. r
5. a
6. k
7. h
a. s
9. b
10. f
11. n
12. d
13. l
14. o
15. p
16. j
17. q
18. false
19. false
20. true
21. false
22. false
23. true
24. true
25. false
26. true
27. true
28. false
29. Jesse Stuart
30. Any order:
    a. illustrative
    b. analytical
    c. argumentative
31. "Sinners in the Hands of an Angry God"
32. diary
33. Bible
34. Either order:
    a. Corrie ten Boom
    b. Jonathan Edwards
35. Any order:
    a. simile
    b. metaphor
    c. personification
    d. hyperbole
36. Either order:
    a. write the classification or category it belongs to
    b. explain the differences between that term and others belonging to the same category

37. that which explains, informs, or gives personal opinions
38. that which pictures a scene, event, or person by use of graphic details
39. one which breaks down a process or situation into its component parts
40. clearness, conciseness, coherence, and completeness
41. logic; the proper sequence of happenings or thought

ALTERNATE LIFEPAC TEST

1. h
2. l
3. g
4. j
5. b
6. c
7. o
8. e
9. a
10. i
11. n
12. d
13. k
14. f
15. c
16. a
17. b
18. b
19. a
20. d
21. c
22. a
23. c
24. a
25. d
26. true
27. true
28. false
29. false
30. true
31. true
32. true
33. false
34. true
35. false
36. Either order:
    a. exposition
    b. description
37. Either order:
    a. formal
    b. informal
38. Either order:
    a. magazines
    b. newspapers
39. editorials
40. anthology
41. Either order:
    a. Thoreau
    b. Emerson
42. Montaigne

43. Any order:
    a. news and magazine articles
    b. biographies
    c. sermons
       or essays, diaries, journals, letters, autobiographies

LANGUAGE ARTS 1106
ALTERNATE LIFEPAC TEST

NAME _____

DATE _____

SCORE _____

Match these items (each answer, 2 points).

1. _____ Francis Bacon
2. _____ a famous example of hyperbole
3. _____ *The Federalist Papers*
4. _____ biography
5. _____ essay
6. _____ character sketches
7. _____ *A True Relation*
8. _____ fiction
9. _____ Corrie ten Boom
10. _____ the novel
11. _____ Carl Sandburg
12. _____ Addison and Steele
13. _____ autobiography
14. _____ "Sinners in the Hands of an Angry God"

a. *The Hiding Place*
b. a written attempt to express an idea
c. vignettes
d. two Englishmen who popularized the essay
e. narrative prose
f. Jonathan Edwards's famous sermon
g. Alexander Hamilton and James Madison
h. the first English essayist
i. a genre of fiction
j. the life story of an individual
k. the story of one's own life
l. the Paul Bunyan stories
m. Benjamin Franklin
n. author of Abraham Lincoln's biography
o. first book written in America

Write the correct letter on each line (each answer, 2 points).

15. A type of figurative language using exaggeration is _____ .
    a. simile   b. metaphor   c. hyperbole   d. personification

16. Expository writing that proves a particular viewpoint or belief follows the _____ pattern of composition.
    a. argumentative   b. analytical   c. illustrative   d. descriptive

17. Nonfiction today is chiefly important as _____ .
    a. an entertainment   b. a source of information
    c. propaganda   d. a description

18. The country that has the world's largest circulation of newspapers is _____ .
    a. United States   b. India   c. Great Britain   d. China

19. A direct comparison between two unlike things is called a(n) _____ .
    a. metaphor   b. simile   c. analysis   d. image

20. Personification gives _____ qualities to inanimate objects or ideas.
    a. descriptive   b. abstract   c. real   d. human

21. A type of essay generally delivered orally that is persuasive in style is a _____ .
    a. journal   b. diary   c. sermon   d. biography

22. Benjamin Franklin was one of many famous Americans who wrote essays in the form of _____ .
    a. letters   b. diaries   c. sermons   d. histories

23. An early American diarist who wrote an account of the Puritan voyage to America was _____ .
    a. Joseph Addison   b. Francis Bacon   c. William Bradford d. Benjamin Franklin

24. A famous early American who wrote his own autobiography was _____ .
    a. Benjamin Franklin b. Thomas Jefferson c. Thomas Paine   d. Richard Steele

25. In developing a nonfiction composition, you should first organize a point-by-point _____ .
    a. argument   b. paragraph   c. description   d. outline

Answer *true* **or** *false* (each answer, 2 points).

26. _____ The purpose of nonfiction is to instruct and inform.

27. _____ Nonfiction is a type of writing that is considered truthful, factual, and real, and that presents an actual situation.

28. _____ Clarity, unity, and conciseness are the three general characteristics of propaganda.

29. _____ Figurative language is used chiefly in expository persuasion.

30. _____ A simile is a kind of figurative language used in descriptive prose.

31. _____ Fiction is narrative prose whose purpose is to entertain.

32. _____ Increased leisure time has helped popularize nonfiction as a source of information.

33. _____ Early American essays were very different from their English counterparts.

34. _____ The illustrative pattern explains something through the use of example or definition.

35. _____ Only one method for organizing an outline is correct.

Complete these statements (each answer, 2 points).

36. Two forms of writing nonfiction include a. _____ and

    b. _____ .

37. The two different forms essays can take are a. _____ and

    b. _____ .

38. Two of the most popular forms of nonfiction in this country today are

    a. _____ and b. _____ .

39. Newspaper articles that present a particular viewpoint or support a certain opinion are

    _____ .

40. A(n) _____ magazine reprints articles from many other sources.

41. Two of the greatest thinkers in America who wrote excellent expository prose were

    a. _____ and b. _____ .

42. The French writer, _____ , first used the word *essai* for his nonfiction writing.

43. Three kinds of nonfiction being written in America today are a. _____ ,

    b. _____ , and c. _____ .

LANGUAGE ARTS 1107

Unit 7: American Drama

TEACHER NOTES

MATERIALS NEEDED FOR LIFEPAC	
Required	Suggested
• Wilder, Thornton. *Our Town*.	• *World Book* or other encyclopedia • King James Version (KJV) of the Bible and/or other versions as permitted • Picozzi, Raymond. *Plays to Enjoy*, or another collection of plays **Reference materials can be in printed, online, or digital formats.*

In this LIFEPAC, the student will study the development of dramatic theater as well as the art of drama itself. The history of drama examines this genre of literature from early times to the present with a specific focus on the growth of theater in America from colonial beginnings well into the twentieth century. The art of drama is discussed by first defining the term drama and explaining its purpose, and then by breaking down a play into its various elements. Included is a step-by-step method for reading and comprehending any play and a detailed examination of one great American drama, Thornton Wilder's *Our Town*.

EXTENDED WRITING ASSIGNMENT

Refer to the 1101 section of this Teacher's Guide for the specific grading procedures described under "Extended Writing Assignment." Also check to see that the students are using at least some of the writing techniques and constructions covered by earlier LIFEPACs in this course. In this specific assignment, grading will depend upon which method the student chooses to present his paper. A scene from a play should, of course, be composed in proper dramatic form and be mechanically correct as well. Originality is a very important element and should be encouraged. If the student chooses the essay, check for organization of material, logical development of theme, and the use of evidence from the text of the play to support the statements in the paper. Students should learn the importance of documenting their ideas through evidence within the play itself.

Again, use the grading guidelines in the 1101 section. Also refer to the essay grading process described in the activity just prior to this one. Additionally, in this paper make sure that the student's Biblical support is correct and that their composition is a logical presentation of the material. Perhaps a brief outline might be helpful here in this organization of material.

ADDITIONAL LEARNING ACTIVITIES

Section 1: The Development of Drama

1. Stage a scene or two from one of the morality plays of the Middle Ages (*Everyman* is the best known and probably the most easily obtained). After the staging, lead a class discussion on the similarities and differences between this kind of play and a modern drama such as *Our Town*.

2. Divide the class evenly into three groups. Assign the first group a Shakespeare scene; the second, a miracle or mystery play of the Middle Ages; and the third, a scene from a Greek drama. Let each group present their scene before the rest of the class.

3. Now that the students have been exposed to several different kinds of drama from several periods of history, let each student pick their favorite of the three and write a brief paper (around 250 words) comparing and contrasting this form with drama today. Students should make sure to address *Our Town* in their paper.

Section 2: The Art of Drama

1. As a class, go through the play *Our Town* and point out the seven basic elements of drama within this particular work. (Example: the characters are Emily, George, etc.; the theme is "Take good heed to the living," and so on.)

2. The purpose of drama is to reflect, criticize, and interpret life. Using this purpose as a basis of discussion, organize a panel within the class to evaluate Wilder's play and point out how it accomplishes these purposes.

3. Let each student take the play *Our Town* and diagram the action to fit into the structure of a play chart given in Figure 1.

Section 3: Wilder's *Our Town*

1. After students have finished reading the play, lead a class discussion about Wilder's expressionistic and symbolic devices (such as the ladders representing upstairs, the chairs representing graves, or the paper boy throwing imaginary papers). Teachers may choose to stage the entire play or at least a complete act if classroom time permits. (Do this activity only after all the students have finished reading the play.)

2. Divide the students into three panels and assign the following topics, one to each:
   a. Wilder's universal theme and how he brings it out in his play.
   b. The setting of the play and how it contributes to the play's universal meaning.
   c. The lack of conventional scenery and how this lack contributes to the universal meaning.

3. Choose another play (a Shakespearian play, a Greek drama, a modern work like *The Miracle Worker*, or an older play like *Everyman*) and then do one of three things with that choice:
   a. Fit the action of that play into the diagram of a play's structure in Figure 1.
   b. Pick out the theme of the play, point out where it is stated in the text, and then paraphrase that theme.
   c. Go through the four fundamental steps in reading a play and apply those steps to this play.

Bible Memory Verses

Section 1
Genesis chapters 6, 7, 8, and 9—the story of Noah, one of the many mystery plays of the Middle Ages

Section 2
Ephesians 4:29—the purpose of drama or literature

Section 3
1 Corinthians 13:12—universal truth or meaning

Administer the LIFEPAC Test.

The test is to be administered in one session. Give no help except with directions.
Evaluate the tests and review areas where the students have done poorly.
Review the pages and activities that stress the concepts tested.
If necessary, administer the Alternate LIFEPAC Test.

ANSWER KEY

SECTION 1

1.1   Greece
1.2   primitive religious rites
1.3   secular
1.4   church
1.5   Any order:
a. mystery
b. morality
c. miracle plays
1.6   established as an acceptable and valuable literary genre
1.7   true
1.8   false
1.9   false
1.10 true
1.11 false
1.12 Any order:
a. Puritans outlawed drama in New England
b. a lack of finances
c. no established audience
d. prejudice against drama as part of court life or monarchs
1.13 Either order:
a. romantic literary style
b. realistic vernacular style
1.14 His adaptation was a melodrama, success-fully combining realistic vernacular used by lower class characters and poetic language used by the upper class ones. His subject, slavery, was a contemporary issue.
1.15 Any order:
a. movement toward realism
b. treatment of serious subjects
c. use of symbolism
1.16 false
1.17 false
1.18 true
1.19 true
1.20 Eugene O'Neill
1.21 realism
1.22 symbolism
1.23 expressionism
1.24 b
1.25 f
1.26 d
1.27 e
1.28 a

1.29 Any order:
a. William Inge
b. Edward Albee
c. Tennessee Williams
d. Arthur Miller
1.30 Any order:
a. Broadway
b. legitimate theater
c. motion picture
d. television
e. little theaters
f. university theaters
g. regional theaters
h. repertory theaters

SELF TEST 1

1.01 b
1.02 i
1.03 e
1.04 g
1.05 l
1.06 j
1.07 h
1.08 a
1.09 k
1.010 f
1.011 a. the colonial period
b. the period after the Revolution
c. the period between 1865 and 1914
d. the early twentieth century (1914–1940)
e. the theater today
1.012 Either order:
a. the romantic literary style
b. the realistic vernacular style
1.013 stage "Yankee"
1.014 George L. Aiken's
1.015 Either order:
a. revival of dramatic literature in Europe
b. the growth of "little theater" in the United States
1.016 Any order:
a. Eugene O'Neill
b. Maxwell Anderson
c. Elmer Rice
1.017 d
1.018 a
1.019 c
1.020 c
1.021 The Puritans outlawed drama in New England. America had no funds for drama and no established audience. Americans were still prejudiced against theater as being immoral because it had been associated with the King.
1.022 Any five:
commercial theater takes the form of Broadway (long-run, popular plays), legitimate theater (short-run, low-budget), motion pictures and television, little theater, university theater, regional theater, and repertory theater

SECTION 2

2.1 Teacher check
2.2 a. a type of play dealing with serious events in which the protagonist is defeated
b. a type of play written to amuse; it ends happily
2.3 Any order:
a. reflects life
b. criticizes life
c. interprets life
2.4 Any order:
a. by exploring the human condition through mirroring reality
b. by providing a platform for examining man's moral and social values
c. by extending human experience in solving social conflicts, moral problems, and personal situations through a make-believe medium of the play
2.5 c
2.6 a
2.7 c
2.8 b
2.9 d
2.10 a
2.11 d
2.12 4
2.13 6
2.14 2
2.15 3
2.16 1
2.17 5
2.18 true
2.19 false
2.20 false
2.21 true
2.22 false
2.23 true
2.24 false
2.25 Teacher check
2.26 performed
2.27 Either order:
a. using your imagination
b. paying careful attention to all the clues and information revealed in the play

2.28 Any order:
a. reading the list of characters
b. identifying the characters and their relationships with each other (understanding the character)
c. noticing the setting or scene (picturing the setting)
d. picking out clues in the dialogue

2.29 Knowledge of the process will make it easier and more enjoyable. Through reading plays, which are often an imitation of reality, the student can learn about the world and about himself.

SELF TEST 2

2.01 c
2.02 f
2.03 m
2.04 d
2.05 k
2.06 i
2.07 l
2.08 h
2.09 b
2.010 j
2.011 g
2.012 e
2.013 Any order:
a. the set
b. the lighting
c. the location of actors
2.014 stage directions
2.015 incident
2.016 conflict
2.017 climax
2.018 resolution
2.019 You should first examine the list of characters. Try to identify the characters and understand their relationships. Picture the setting or scenery. Pick out clues in the dialogue as you read.
2.020 A play usually begins with exposition. An incident occurs, creating a problem. The ensuing struggle or conflict (rising action) reaches a turning point or climax. The falling action leads to the resolution or explanation of the play's action.
2.021 a
2.022 c
2.023 b
2.024 a
2.025 a type of popular character representing the American whose native wit can outsmart the sophisticated foreigner
2.026 large commercial productions in New York with long-run, popular plays
2.027 a thin backdrop curtain which becomes transparent when lit from behind
2.028 a group of actors that produces a variety of types of plays
2.029 Any order:
a. Puritans outlawed it
b. no funds
c. no audience
d. prejudice against anything associated with the monarchy

2.030 Any order:
- a. Arthur Miller
- b. Clifford Odets
- c. Maxwell Anderson
- d. Eugene O'Neill
- or Lillian Hellman, Elmer Rice, Edward Albee, Thornton Wilder, William Inge, Tennessee Williams

SECTION 3

3.1 Madison, Wisconsin
3.2 China
3.3 teacher of French
3.4 *The Bridge of San Luis Rey*
3.5 *Our Town*
3.6 "man has a dignity and a destiny"
3.7 innovator
3.8 true
3.9 false
3.10 true
3.11 true
3.12 false
3.13 true
3.14 true
3.15 true
3.16 false
3.17 true
3.18 7
2
6
1
10
3
5
9
8
4
3.19 Any order:
- a. "get's wonderful bright"
- b. "down in the holla"
- c. "over yonder"
- d. "the hull town"
- e. "s' far as"
3.20 Any order:
- a. He actually sets the stage.
- b. He speaks directly to the audience as a narrator, explaining and introducing.
- c. He speaks to the characters and speaks for an unseen character.
3.21 Any order:
- a. woman in the balcony who questions Mr. Webb
- b. belligerent man in the back of the auditorium
- c. lady in a box seat
3.22 d
3.23 b
3.24 g
3.25 f
3.26 a
3.27 l
3.28 h

3.29   k

3.30   e

3.31   j

3.32   Either order:
  a. the statement that Dr. Gibbs died in 1930
  b. the statement that Joe Crowell, Jr., the paperboy, graduated at the head of his class, got a scholarship, and died in France during the war

3.33   three years

3.34   Either order:
  a. he describes Mrs. Gibbs and Mrs. Webb as they begin breakfast
  b. Howie Newsom is still delivering the milk

3.35   French toast

3.36   State Agriculture College

3.37   Morgan's drugstore

3.38   Mrs. Soames

3.39   Either order:
  a. not wanting to grow up
  b. fearing they can never be perfect

3.40   Most adolescents have mixed feelings and doubts about growing up. They want to be as nearly perfect as possible, yet doubt that they can.

3.41   Examples; any order:
  a. Mrs. Gibbs fears the couple is too young—she cries.
  b. Dr. Gibbs finds it hard to accept his son as an adult. He tells that he thought he was marrying a stranger.
  c. Mrs. Webb cries.
  d. George complains everyone is pushing him and all he wants to do is "be a fella."
  e. Emily says she has never felt so alone, says she hates George, wishes she were dead, and calls her father.

3.42   She keeps praising the beauty of the wedding and emphasizing happiness. She is more of a type than a fully-developed character and probably represents the "busybody" nature of some people. Since most audiences are familiar with the words of a traditional ceremony, the audience did not need to hear them.

3.43   Teacher check

3.44   Any order:
  a. Dr. Gibbs says everyone has troubles.
  b. Mrs. Gibbs says people were meant to be married.
  c. Mr. Webb tells George the advice his father gave him concerning the roles of husband and wife.
  d. Mrs. Webb laments that girls are unprepared for marriage.
  e. Mr. Webb asks George to take care of his daughter.
  f. Emily expresses the need for love.
  g. Mrs. Soames expresses the search for happiness.

3.45   false

3.46   true

3.47   false

3.48   true

3.49   true

3.50   false

3.51   true

3.52   true

3.53   true

3.54   Student check

3.55   Teacher check

3.56   Teacher check

SELF TEST 3

3.01 g
3.02 a
3.03 i
3.04 d
3.05 b
3.06 e
3.07 k
3.08 h
3.09 f
3.010 c
3. 011 d
3.012 b
3.013 d
3.014 b
3.015 a
3.016 Joe Crowell, Jr.
3.017 protagonist
3.018 resolution
3.019 a play
3.020 the climax
3.021 Either order:
        a. internal
        b. external
3.022 exposition
3.023 plot
3.024 style
3.025 theme
3.026 Three years have passed. Joe Crowell, Jr. is no longer the paperboy. George and Emily have fallen in love and are getting married.
3.027 Nine years have passed. Emily has given birth to two children and has died. Mrs. Gibbs, Mrs. Soames, and others have died.
3.028 Man struggles against change, yet can do nothing to stop the progress of life and its accompanying changes.
3.029 Man cannot appreciate the real beauty of life and savor each tiny moment until he has lost life.

LIFEPAC TEST

1. d
2. a
3. f
4. b
5. e
6. c
7. h
8. i
9. Any order:
   a. plot
   b. character
   c. theme
   d. style
   e. setting
   f. structure
   g. stage direction
10. Any order:
    a. understanding the characters
    b. picturing the setting
    c. picking out clues
11. Pulitzer Prizes
12. a technique used to show previous actions or situations
13. the school of writing which describes things as they seem to the author, not as they should or could be
14. the quality of applying to or having shared by all people
15. the design or pattern of a play
16. the main character who has to struggle against the forces opposing them
17. a playwright and novelist who won three Pulitzer Prizes
18. a
19. d
20. b
21. d

ALTERNATE LIFEPAC TEST

1. f
2. h
3. a
4. g
5. c
6. j
7. b
8. d
9. e
10. k
11. b
12. a
13. d
14. c
15. a
16. d
17. b
18. a
19. d
20. c
21. a
22. b
23. c
24. d
25. b
26. true
27. false
28. true
29. true
30. false
31. false
32. true
33. true
34. true
35. false

LANGUAGE ARTS 1107
ALTERNATE LIFEPAC TEST

NAME _____

DATE _____

SCORE _____

Match these items (each answer, 3 points).

1. _____ Eugene O'Neill
2. _____ Harriet Beecher Stowe
3. _____ mystery play
4. _____ protagonist
5. _____ climax
6. _____ characters
7. _____ the stage manager
8. _____ *Everyman*
9. _____ the cemetery scene
10. _____ Grover's Corners, New Hampshire

a. a re-enactment of a Bible story

b. guide and narrator for *Our Town*

c. turning point of a play

d. a morality play of the Middle Ages

e. Act III of *Our Town*

f. America's first great playwright

g. the main character of a play

h. *Uncle Tom's Cabin*

i. William Shakespeare

j. the people involved in the action of a play

k. the setting of *Our Town*

Write the letter for the correct answer on the line (each answer, 3 points).

11. The earliest written dramas that have survived to today come from _____ .
a. England   b. Greece   c. Rome   d. ancient times

12. The time and place of the action of a play is its _____ .
a. setting   b. theme   c. climax   d. conflict

13. The opening material that introduces the characters and situation of a play is the _____ .
a. dialogue   b. action   c. conflict   d. exposition

14. The Stage Manager's long speech that provides the exposition for the play in the opening

scene is an example of a _____ .
   a. theme   b. climax   c. monologue   d. resolution

15. The first step in reading a play is to _____ .
   a. understand the characters   b. find the climax
   c. look for clues in the dialogue   d. study the stage setting

16. *Our Town* can be classified as a modern _____ play.
   a. miracle   b. mystery   c. classic   d. morality

17. "Take good heed to the living" is one way of stating the moral or the _____ of the play *Our
Town*.
   a. conflict   b. theme   c. rising action   d. characterization

18. Wilder chose a rural lifestyle in a small New England town at the turn of the century because

his goal was _____ .
   a. simplicity   b. financial   c. historical   d. reality

19. The two lovers of *Our Town* are _____ .
   a. Mr. and Mrs. Gibbs   b. the doctor and Emily
   c. Bessie and Howie   d. Emily and George

20. A technique of taking an audience back in time during the action of a play is called _____ .
   a. expressionism   b. dialogue   c. flashback   d. realism

21. The series of events that make up the actual story of a play is its _____ .
   a. plot   b. dialogue   c. setting   d. theme

22. The final "working out of the plot" that explains what happened and why is the _____ .
   a. climax   b. resolution   c. exposition   d. monologue

23. Informal speech used by a certain people or a certain country is called _____ .
   a. dialogue   b. formal English   c. vernacular   d. paraphrase

24. The Stage Manager assumes various small _____ during the course of the play.
   a. actions   b. settings   c. conflicts   d. roles

25. The speeches of the various characters in a play are the _____ .
   a. satire   b. dialogue   c. action   d. theme

Answer *true* **or** *false* (each answer, 2 points).

26. _____ The problem the protagonist must solve during the play is the conflict.

27. _____ William Shakespeare was a famous playwright of the Middle Ages.

28. _____ Expressionism, realism, and symbolism were three schools of playwriting in the twentieth century in America.

29. _____ Eight different kinds of theater exist in America today.

30. _____ Early Roman drama was religious in nature.

31. _____ Morality plays are based on the lives of the saints.

32. _____ Thornton Wilder won three Pulitzer Prizes in his lifetime.

33. _____ In order to read a play properly, one must stage the play in one's own imagination.

34. _____ *Our Town* employs devices from several different schools of playwrighting.

35. _____ The universal theme of *Our Town* is stated by George in the end.

LANGUAGE ARTS 1108

Unit 8: Studies in the American Novel

TEACHER NOTES

MATERIALS NEEDED FOR LIFEPAC	
Required	Suggested
• Hemingway, Ernest. *The Old Man and the Sea.*	• *World Book* or other encyclopedia • King James Version (KJV) of the Bible and/or other versions as permitted • Hawthorne, Nathaniel. *The Scarlet Letter*. • Steinbeck, John. *The Pearl*. • Twain, Mark. *The Adventures of Huckleberry Finn*. • a library copy of a biography of one of the authors listed: Tarkington, Cather, Wharton. **Reference materials can be in printed, online, or digital formats.*

In this LIFEPAC, the student will study the history and development of the American novel and examine in detail one specific work, Ernest Hemingway's *The Old Man and the Sea*. The history of the novel is divided into three time periods: the eighteenth century, the nineteenth century, and the twentieth century.

Discussed in the final section of this LIFEPAC is the definition and purpose of a critical essay and the art of writing such an essay. Exercises applying that art to the analysis of Hemingway's novel are also included.

EXTENDED WRITING ASSIGNMENT

This essay must first be graded mechanically according to the guidelines in this Teacher's Guide (1101). The organization of material, logical transition from point to point, and step-by-step development (according to the outline) of the thesis should all be considered.

1. Recheck definitions of metaphor and symbol.

2. See if the symbolic meanings destroy the literal meanings (if they do they are incorrect).

3. Be sure that the symbolic and metaphoric meanings do not distort the text of the Bible or the novel.

4. Check the point of view in the student's thesis. The students are permitted to write about and support their own opinion, but they should leave out personal pronouns.

ADDITIONAL LEARNING ACTIVITIES

Section 1: The American Novel

1. Obtain from the library or from public domain versions online, a copy of one of the first novels (Richardson's *Pamela* or another early novel) and read aloud a few brief passages (particularly the beginning) to the class.

2. Read selections from a novel that was published later than the novel from activity 1 (but not a modern novel).

3. Using the oral reading in the teacher-directed activity as a basis, organize a panel discussion comparing and contrasting the older works with Hemingway's modern novel.

    Examples:
    a. The older style is much stiffer, more formal, more flowery.
    b. The author often intrudes directly into his work and addresses the "Dear Reader."

4. Students who read quickly may choose one of the three novels in the suggested literature, read it outside of class, and then prepare an outline for an oral report to the class on one of the following topics:

    a. The imagery used in the novel.
    b. The Christian significance (if any) of the story.
    c. The differences in this work and *The Old Man and the Sea*.

Section 2: *The Old Man and the Sea*

1. Hemingway once said that the King James Version of the Bible contained some of the greatest prose in literature. His particular favorites were Samuel, Kings, and Chronicles. Using the text of *The Old Man and the Sea*, go over in class passages in the novel that reflect this statement. (Note: some may have been brought out in the LIFEPAC exercises in this section.)

2. *The Old Man and the Sea* is filled with Christian imagery. Organize a class discussion based on this imagery that brings out at least the more obvious images. Make certain that the students are identifying the meanings behind the images as well as the images themselves. (This discussion may help them with the critical analysis paper required in Section 3.)

3. Students who work more slowly may benefit from learning more about one of the authors mentioned in this LIFEPAC. (Examples: Hawthorne or Cooper)

4. Hemingway used all the basic elements of a novel—plot, characterization, and mood—in his work. Assign students to write a brief plot summary, character sketch, or mood analysis on *The Old Man and the Sea*.

Section 3: The Critical Essay

1. Choose a good critical essay and read parts of it aloud to the class. Possible choices might include William Dean Howell's "Criticism and Fiction," Henry James' "The Art of Fiction," or T.S. Eliot's "Tradition and the Individual Talent." If time allows, the entire essay should be read. In any case, parts read should be explained.

2. Using the preceding essay, organize a group or class discussion on the points made by the author and try to apply them to Hemingway's novel. Consider these questions: Did

Hemingway follow the critics' advice in writing his novel? In what ways does this book fit into (or not fit into) the critical pattern discussed in class?

3. Write a brief paper summarizing the points brought out in the group discussion.

4. Advanced students might choose another critical essay and write a brief paper covering the same points about novels that were discussed in class. Possibilities are:

   a. Either of the two not chosen for the class reading and discussion.
   b. Virginia Woolf's "How Should One Read a Book?"
   c. T.S. Eliot's "Religion and Literature"
   d. Edgar Allen Poe's "The Poetic Principle"
   e. Walt Whitman's "Democratic Vistas"
   f. Emile Zola's "The Experimental Novel"

Bible Memory Verses

Section 1
Revelation 20:12—books

Section 2
Psalm 90:10—days are numbered

Section 3
2 Timothy 6:18 and 19—rewards of goodness
2 Samuel 22:28—afflicted will be saved but haughty will be brought down

Administer the LIFEPAC Test.

The test is to be administered in one session. Give no help except with directions.
Evaluate the tests and review areas where the students have done poorly.
Review the pages and activities that stress the concepts tested.
If necessary, administer the Alternate LIFEPAC Test.

ANSWER KEY

SECTION 1

1.1 false
1.2 true
1.3 true
1.4 false
1.5 true
1.6 b
1.7 a
1.8 b
1.9 a
1.10 c
1.11 Any order:
a. *Deerslayer*
b. *Last of the Mohicans*
c. *Pathfinder*
d. *Pioneers*
e. *Prairie*
1.12 Any order:
a. *The Two Admirals*
b. *Red Rover*
c. *Redskins*
or *Wing-and-Wing,
Afloat and Ashore,
Miles Wallingford*
1.13 Any order:
a. *Satanstoe*
b. *Chainbearer*
c. *Redskins*
1.14 He used many forms well and opened new territories for fiction. His description of men was important to the development of characters. He wrote some of the first truly delightful American novels.
1.15 storyteller
1.16 Sir Walter Scott
1.17 romancer
1.18 symbol
1.19 sketches
1.20 *The House of Seven Gables*
1.21 Example:
Simms thought carefully about the nature of fiction, the use of history in fiction, the difference between the novel and the romance, and the relationship of both these forms to morals and life.
1.22 Edmund Spenser and John Bunyan
1.23 Teacher check

1.24 Either order:
a. *Typee*
b. *Omoo*
1.25 Any order:
a. *Moby-Dick*
b. *Billy Budd*
c. *Mardi*
or *Redburn,
White-Jacket,
Pierre*
1.26 *Uncle Tom's Cabin*
1.27 Any order:
a. *Mardi*
b. *Moby-Dick*
c. *Billy Budd*
1.28 d
1.29 a
1.30 f
1.31 b
1.32 c
1.33 true
1.34 true
1.35 true
1.36 false
1.37 true
1.38 Example:
developed the art of the storyteller; contributed important social and political criticism; created memorable characters; contributed to the romantic revival
1.39 Any order:
a. domestic situations
b. Civil War
c. temperance
d. pioneer life
e. the Old South (pre-Civil War)
or religion; realism
1.40 a. Stephen Crane
b. Elizabeth Wetherell
c. Louisa May Alcott
d. Hamlin Garland
e. Frank Norris
1.41 k
1.42 f
1.43 a
1.44 j
1.45 c

1.46	h
1.47	b
1.48	e
1.49	g
1.50	d
1.51	Teacher check

SELF TEST 1

1.01	true
1.02	true
1.03	true
1.04	false
1.05	true
1.06	true
1.07	true
1.08	false
1.09	false
1.010	true
1.011	d
1.012	g
1.013	c
1.014	h
1.015	k
1.016	f
1.017	b
1.018	i
1.019	e
1.020	a
1.021	c
1.022	a
1.023	c
1.024	b
1.025	c
1.026	a
1.027	b
1.028	c
1.029	a
1.030	c

1.031 Either order:
a. *The Prince and the Pauper*
b. *A Connecticut Yankee in King Arthur's Court*

1.032 *McTeague*

1.033 gothic

1.034 Any order:
a. *The Deerslayer*
b. *The Last of the Mohicans*
c. *The Pathfinder*

1.035 *Arrowsmith*

1.036 idealist

1.037 *The Scarlet Letter*

1.038 social history

1.039 *The Bridge of San Luis Rey*

1.040 Example:
developed art of story telling; social and political criticism; romantic revival

1.041 Example:
hearth and home; usually concerned with tragic occurrences; usually sentimental

1.042 Example:
Christian attitudes and ideals; use of symbols

SECTION 2

2.1 death
2.2 Any order:
    a. spare
    b. direct
    c. frequently uses "and"
2.3 Either order:
    a. horrible
    b. tragic
2.4 a. impression
    b. words
2.5 a sense of order
2.6 interrelated actions
2.7 the climax
2.8 Any order:
    a. planned order of events by author
    b. a series of actions that lead logically to the end of the story
    c. conflict of forces must take place
2.9 Any order:
    a. he artificially orders events
    b. he chooses the end of the novel
    c. he focuses life by selecting events, actions, characters
2.10 c
2.11 a
2.12 b
2.13 Any order:
    a. block of information
    b. through action
    c. from within
2.14 mood, tone or a work established by setting, character, action, emotion
2.15 direct the attitudes and expectations of the reader
2.16 a particular, concrete appeal to the senses, to the experience of the senses, or to the memory of experience
2.17 an image that does not change or extend. the obvious meaning of the words
2.18 an image that involves a "turn" on the literal meaning of the word
2.19 Examples; any order:
    a. bottom p. 9 – top p. 10
    b. bottom p. 12
    c. bottom p. 15 – top p. 16
    d. bottom p. 18 – top p. 19
    e. top p. 29
2.20 Teacher check; answers will vary. Answers must include both reference and specific example of imagery.

2.21 true
2.22 false
2.23 true
2.24 false
2.25 false
2.26 false
2.27 collection of images in a work
2.28 repetition of images many times not consciously cultivated that lead to deeper meaning of the work
2.29 actual intent carried in words of opposite meaning
2.30 Example:
His genius carries all the attributes of his unknown ancestors, and who should want to know them?
2.31 A symbol is itself and stands for or means something else.
2.32 An allegory gives a hidden meaning to the characters, settings, and events, and it has a fixed meaning.
2.33 A metaphor evokes an object so that an idea or quality may be demonstrated.
2.34 An analogy is a comparison of two things that are alike in certain respects.
2.35 f
2.36 a
2.37 d
2.38 e
2.39 b
2.40 a. different from other creatures
    b. created by God
    c. fish—subject to God's will
    d. man has dominion over
    e. fish story; fish used as God's instrument
    f. healing
    g. fish used to pay temple tax
2.41 a. poor are needy
    b. a poor person is an unfortunate one
    c. poor in spirit
    d. Quotes list various ways in which the poor are understood and treated in the Bible as the special charges of God.
2.42 Examples:
    a. the old man's youth
    b. to find one's life
    c. to be in life
    d. to find one's own resources
2.43 Teacher check

SELF TEST 2

2.01 true
2.02 true
2.03 true
2.04 false
2.05 false
2.06 true
2.07 false
2.08 true
2.09 true
2.010 true
2.011 f
2.012 k
2.013 a
2.014 i
2.015 c
2.016 g
2.017 b
2.018 e
2.019 h
2.020 d
2.021 c
2.022 a
2.023 a
2.024 b
2.025 c
2.026 b
2.027 b
2.028 c
2.029 a
2.030 "turn"
2.031 author's
2.032 alike
2.033 Any order:
a. artificially ordering events
b. choosing an end of the novel
c. selecting events, actions, or characters
2.034 Any order:
a. by using blocks of information
b. through action
c. from within
2.035 Either order:
a. tone
b. atmosphere
2.036 an image that does not change or extend the obvious meaning of the words
2.037 actual intent is carried in words of the opposite meaning
2.038 repetition of images many times not consciously cultivated that lead to deeper meaning of a work
2.039 man, boy, sea, fish

SECTION 3

3.1 Example: The goal of interpretation is to discover what the author is saying; that is, the meaning of the parts and the whole.
3.2 Answers will vary.
3.3 he is an ascetic: wrinkles, creases, in the sun, poor, silent, throughout book
3.4 The bird was a sign of where life was in the sun; also an ancient sign of wisdom pp. 34–35, 37.
3.5 He uses the colors of majesty (purple, deep blue) to describe it throughout book.
3.6 Each is beautiful, but disguises a serious danger; temptation pp. 35–36.
3.7 Teacher check

3.8 through 3.10
Hint: The purpose of these activities is for the student to display initiative and understanding in using the Bible to evaluate a situation. Correct answers must include at least one example from the book of either the boy's or old man's attitude toward the subject and at least one Bible reference to demonstrate God's attitude concerning the same subject. The teacher should review these activities when checking 3.12–3.15.

3.11 Hint: Any answer substantiated with examples or quotes from the book could be correct. Example: The old man's attitude toward God is very superficial. He thinks of God only in times of suffering and tries to appease God by offering mechanical, vain prayers. God is neither superficial (Col.1:15–20) nor can he be appeased by vain, repetitious prayers (Matt. 6:7).
3.12 Teacher check
3.13 Teacher check
3.14 Teacher check
3.15 Teacher check

SELF TEST 3

3.01   true
3.02   false
3.03   true
3.04   true
3.05   false
3.06   false
3.07   false
3.08   true
3.09   true
3.010 true
3.011 j
3.012 f
3.013 k
3.014 a
3.015 i
3.016 e
3.017 b
3.018 g
3.019 d
3.020 h
3.021 How does the writer say it?
3.022 Was what the writer said worthwhile?
3.023 meaning
3.024 a. Leatherstocking
       b. James Fenimore Cooper
3.025 Any order:
       a. man
       b. boy
       c. fish
       d. sea
3.026 the old man's youth
3.027 Either order:
       a. deep blue
       b. purple
3.028 Either order:
       a. the old man's life
       b. existence of all life
3.029 Example: someone who could be turned to in times of suffering and appeased by the offering of mechanical prayers
3.030 A symbol is itself and stands for or means something else.
3.031 evokes an object so that an idea or conflict may be demonstrated; implied analogy
3.032 collection of images in a work
3.033 wrinkled, creased, tanned, skin cancer, calm
3.034 cares, serves, looks to the old man, polite

LIFEPAC TEST

1. true
2. true
3. true
4. true
5. false
6. false
7. true
8. true
9. true
10. false
11. d
12. h
13. a
14. k
15. c
16. j
17. b
18. i
19. e
20. f
21. a
22. c
23. b
24. c
25. a
26. c
27. a
28. b
29. b
30. c
31. a
32. Any order:
   a. *The Pathfinder*
   b. *The Pioneers*
   c. *The Last of the Mohicans*
33. Any order:
   a. know the text
   b. select a topic
   c. find evidence
   d. outline
   e. write the essay
34. Any order:
   a. interpretation
   b. evaluation
   c. analysis
35. *The Scarlet Letter*
36. Example: The old man's attitude toward God is very superficial. He thinks of God only in times of suffering and tries to appease God by offering mechanical, vain prayers.
37. Example:
   wrinkled, creased, tanned, skin cancer, calm
38. existence, life

ALTERNATE LIFEPAC TEST

1. true
2. false
3. true
4. true
5. true
6. false
7. true
8. false
9. true
10. true
11. h
12. f
13. j
14. a
15. b
16. c
17. k
18. m
19. e
20. d
21. i
22. l
23. Any order:
   a. plot
   b. characterization
   c. mood
24. explication
25. evaluation
26. Any order:
   a. historical
   b. sentimental
   or gothic, epistolary
27. *Innocents Abroad*
28. Herman Melville
29. James Fenimore Cooper
30. Mark Twain
31. b
32. c
33. a
34. c
35. d
36. b
37. a
38. d

LANGUAGE ARTS 1108

ALTERNATE LIFEPAC TEST

NAME _____

DATE _____

SCORE _____

81

101

Answer *true* **or** *false* (each answer, 2 points).

1. _____ Captain Ahab is Melville's chief character in *Moby-Dick*.

2. _____ *Pamela* is a clear-cut choice for the first American novel.

3. _____ The early American novels were novels of sentiment dealing with domestic situations.

4. _____ Many of the early novels were written in the form of letters.

5. _____ The hero of The Leatherstocking Tales is Natty Bumppo.

6. _____ Theodore Dreiser is a fine example of the writers of the historical novel.

7. _____ John Steinbeck's fiction can be considered allegorically as well as literally.

8. _____ *The Scarlet Letter* was written by Herman Melville.

9. _____ Hemingway began his career in fiction with short stories.

10. _____ Images in fiction help to illustrate the meaning of a novel.

Match these items (each answer, 2 points).

11. _____ James Fenimore Cooper

12. _____ William Hill Brown

13. _____ Nathaniel Hawthorne

14. _____ Stephen Crane

15. _____ Ernest Hemingway

16. _____ *Pilgrim's Progress*

17. _____ literary criticism

18. _____ *Charlotte Temple*

19. _____ Mark Twain

20. _____ *A Connecticut Yankee in King Arthur's Court*

21. _____ John Steinbeck

22. _____ William Faulkner

a. *The Red Badge of Courage*

b. *For Whom the Bell Tolls*

c. a very famous allegory

d. example of a novel of satire

e. Samuel Clemens

f. *The Power of Sympathy*

g. *Babbitt*

h. *The Deerslayer*

i. *The Grapes of Wrath*

j. *The Marble Faun*

k. a serious analysis of a literary work

l. Yoknapatawpha County

m. example of a domestic sentimental novel

Complete these statements (each answer, 3 points).

23. The three basic elements of all novels are a. _____ , b. _____ , and c. _____ .

24. The critical process of explaining the difficult aspects of a novel is known as _____ .

25. Determining the value of an author's work is called _____ .

26. Two of the early types of novels were a. _____ and b. _____ .

27. The book that first brought recognition to Mark Twain was _____ _____ .

28. The literary discoverer of the South Seas in the nineteenth century was _____ _____ .

29. The novelist who did most to establish the character of the Native American was _____ _____ .

30. The man considered the dominant personality in nineteenth-century American novels was _____ .

Write the letter for the correct answer on the line (each answer, 3 points).

31. *Modern Chivalry* is an example of a _____ novel.
    a. gothic   b. picaresque   c. historical   d. domestic

32. Harriet Beecher Stowe wrote the very successful novel _____ in 1852.
    a. *Moby-Dick*   b. *Typee*   c. *Uncle Tom's Cabin*   d. *Tom Sawyer*

33. A nineteenth-century champion of the _____ novel was William Dean Howells.
    a. realistic   b. historical   c. sentimental   d. allegory

34. Theodore Dreiser's great realistic novel was _____ .
    a. *Pierre*   b. *Babbitt*
    c. *An American Tragedy*   d. *Main Street*

35. A figure of speech which communicates the writer's intent in words carrying an opposite meaning is_____ .
    a. image   b. metaphor   c. simile   d. irony

36. *Weiland*, by Charles Brockden Brown is an example of a _____ novel.
    a. picaresque   b. gothic   c. historical   d. domestic

37. As a novelist, Hawthorne was greatly influenced by the works of _____ .
    a. Sir Walter Scott   b. Samuel Richardson
    c. James Fenimore Cooper   d. Henry James

38. Edith Wharton's masterpiece was the novel _____ .
    a. *Mardi*   b. *Main Street*
    c. *Of Time and the River*   d. *Ethan Frome*

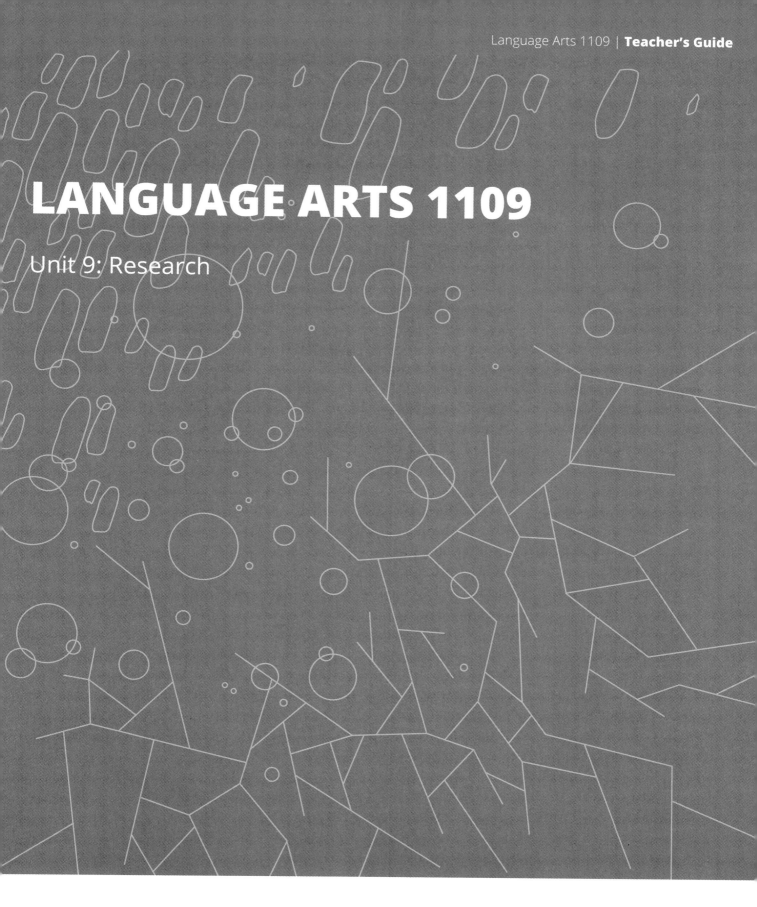

LANGUAGE ARTS 1109

Unit 9: Research

TEACHER NOTES

MATERIALS NEEDED FOR LIFEPAC	
Required	Suggested
(None)	• *World Book Dictionary* or *American Heritage Dictionary* • King James Version (KJV) of the Bible and/or other versions as permitted *Reference materials can be in printed, online, or digital formats.*

A major high school project is often the research paper. Although it can be reduced to merely an inventory and rehashing of other people's ideas set up in a rather formidable—and foreign—structure, the research paper can also be one of the most exciting portions of the curriculum, encouraging original thinking among students while acknowledging debts to previous thinkers. This LIFEPAC presents a detailed approach to the investigative process, helping students choose and limit their subjects, then prepare workable thesis statements. The middle section reviews library sources and suggests methods for taking notes and preparing works cited pages. The third section offers guides for the actual composing process.

Apart from reviewing the use of library and online sources and learning to use the customary methods of a research paper—a necessary tool for any college-bound student—students may derive a great deal of satisfaction from investigating a topic of particular interest to them (perhaps bounded by class studies, but still suggested by the students' own interests). Additionally, they may learn the pleasure of original thinking—building upon other people's ideas (and courteously citing those borrowings) in order to approach a new idea as well as mentally "arguing" with opposing viewpoints as a way of strengthening one's own logic.

EXTENDED WRITING ASSIGNMENT

The research paper will include a title page, a detailed outline, the body of the paper, and the works cited. For basic grading guidelines, refer to this Teacher's Guide (1101) under "Extended Writing Assignment." Look for a controlling thesis and development of that thesis through related topic sentences. Students should show familiarity with citations and provide adequate citations and works cited sources.

ADDITIONAL LEARNING ACTIVITIES

Section 1: The Investigative Process

1. As a class, discuss possible research topics. List these ideas on the board or a poster. Have the students write a possible thesis statement based on a topic of their choice.

2. Divide the class into groups of four or five to work with the poster-based thesis statements. Give a time limit for them to work together to synthesize their ideas and come up with one workable thesis statement per group. Have each group share their idea with the class.

3. Have the student write a one-page essay (about 250 words) about the value of original thinking in a research paper.

Section 2: The Library

1. Have groups work with a favorite parable. They may all choose the same one, or each group may choose a different one. Let them work together to plan a play based on their parable, using library resources to find out what the countryside would have been like, what foods they might be eating at a banquet, what crops they might be cultivating, and so forth.

2. Divide the class into groups of five. Provide each group with a list including words to define, famous persons' names to find in *Who's Who*, countries to list neighbors of from an atlas, and so forth. They may work together any way they choose to complete their list within a time limit. Afterward, see which group got the greatest number correct; discuss any difficulties.

3. Have students choose a topic of interest and find three articles (from the library or reliable online source) about that topic. Assign them to write a brief report about their findings.

Section 3: The Composition

1. Write a broad topic word on the board. Discuss ways to limit it; then, with the class, derive a workable thesis statement. Through questioning, let students volunteer ideas for formulating an outline, then write them into outline form on the board as the discussion progresses so they can see how the outline builds.

2. Divide the class into two groups. Let one volunteer from each group read a favorite parable or Bible story aloud, leaving off the conclusion. Let students write their own conclusions; discuss in groups.

3. Have students create correct citations for the three references previously found (Section 2, Individual Activity). Then, they should combine these into a properly formatted works cited page.

Bible Memory Verses

Section 1
Genesis 3:19—the importance of work
Proverbs 8:1–14—nature is orderly

Section 2
Proverbs 12:25—a good word
Proverbs 15:1—the wise use knowledge rightly
Proverbs 15:23—a word in due season
Proverbs 25:11—a word fitly spoken is like apples of gold

Section 3
1 Timothy 6:17–19—trust in God and do good works, communicate willingly

Administer the LIFEPAC Test.

ANSWER KEY

SECTION 1

1.1   a. not appropriate
        b. appropriate
        c. appropriate
        d. not appropriate
        e. not appropriate

1.2   a. (a) personal experience
        b. (d) biographical subjects do not lend themselves to research
        c. (e) the subject appears to be persuasive and not readily researched

1.3   a. limited
        b. broad
        c. broad
        d. limited
        e. broad

1.4   a. Greek
        b. bark enclosing the pith of the papyrus plant from which paper was made in ancient times; or book
        c. Greek
        d. the books of the Bible officially accepted by both Jews and Christians

1.5   Teacher check

1.6   Examples:
        a. The Bible presents the best, and at times the only, information about certain historical events.
        b. The Bible has influenced people more than any other book ever written.
        c. The canon is made up of the books of the Bible historically accepted by both Jews and Christians.

1.7   Examples:
        a. Teenage marriages are often doomed to failure.
        b. The purpose of this paper is to show that teenage marriages are often doomed to failure.

1.8   Examples:
        a. A cat's eye is similar in many ways to a human eye.
        b. This paper will present three ways in which a cat's eye is similar to a human eye.

1.9   Examples:
        a. My home town is a reflection of big city life.
        b. This paper will demonstrate the ways in which my home town is a big city.

1.10   a. restricted
        b. unrestricted
        c. unrestricted
        d. unrestricted
        e. unrestricted

1.11   Examples:
        b. Painting can be a profitable hobby. (any art form would be satisfactory)
        c. Classical music is the basis for a particular rock song. (Students should name a specific song. Another possible type of sentence would name a feature of classical music and apply it to rock music.)
        d. (The cause needs to be more specific than merely economic.)
        e. Tennis (or any other sport) exercises the mind as well as the body.

1.12   a. not precise
        b. not precise
        c. precise
        d. precise
        e. not precise

1.13   Examples:
        a. Teachers are not always as kind (or strict, or any similar word) as their appearance would suggest.
        b. High school football costs the players hundreds of dollars per year to participate.
        e. Fashion fads become passé in a matter of months. (or something similar)

1.14   a. unified
        b. not unified
        c. unified
        d. not unified
        e. not unified

1.15 Examples:
b. Private school enrollment has increased in the past five years because parents have lost confidence in the public schools.
or
Private school enrollment has increased in the past five years because parents have more to spend on education.
d. Teen magazines are an inexpensive source of well-written fiction (or nonfiction) (or articles—might be too broad, but it is unified)
e. Raising earthworms is a profitable hobby. or Raising earthworms is an enjoyable hobby.

1.16 Teacher check the thesis statement for its relationship to the subject under investigation. Be certain that it is restricted, unified, and precise. The purpose should be a sincere motivation for writing the paper.

SELF TEST 1

1.01 true
1.02 false
1.03 true
1.04 true
1.05 false
1.06 true
1.07 false
1.08 Any order:
a. select
b. analyze
c. evaluate
1.09 the investigative process or research
1.010 broad
1.011 Any order:
a. an encyclopedia
b. a specialized dictionary
c. a biographical encyclopedia or a history, a textbook
1.012 thesis statement
1.013 capable of being researched
1.014 too broad
1.015 adequate
1.016 too broad
1.017 too broad
1.018 too broad
1.019 adequate
1.020 limited
1.021 too broad
1.022 too broad
1.023 (1.014) football equipment, football plays, football fans, football haters, football safety, football for females, etc.
1.024 (1.015) Topic should reflect farming in one state or a specific kind of farming in the Middle Atlantic States.
1.025 (1.017) new careers in the 2020s, a specific career that will be new in the 2020s, computer career possibilities in the 2020s
1.026 (1.018) Native American burial grounds of the Hopi people of Arizona or similar subject
1.027 (1.021) Should name a particular ghost town such as Jerome, Arizona, and mention its history or what it is like today—the rebirth of Jerome, Arizona, for example.
1.028 (1.022) Edible Underwater Plants are the answer to future shortages; any subject that names a specific underwater plant and attempts to

go into detail about it; harvesting of underwater plants

1.029 not precise
1.030 adequate
1.031 adequate
1.032 unrestricted
1.033 not unified
1.034 adequate
1.035 not precise

SECTION 2

2.1 Teacher check

2.2
a. tertiary source
b. secondary source
c. primary source
d. primary source
e. secondary source
f. secondary source
g. primary source
h. secondary source

2. 3
a. I
b. C
c. I
d. I

2.4
a. (a) Porter, J.R. *Jesus Christ: The Jesus of History, the Christ of Faith*. Oxford University Press, 2007.
b. (c) Mortenson, Greg et al. *Three Cups of Tea*. Penguin Group, 2007.
c. (d) Fitzgerald, Scott. *The Great Gatsby*. Simon and Schuster, 2004.

2.5 Teacher should check for correct bibliographical form, library call number, and the annotation.

2.6
a. C
b. I
c. I
d. C

2.7
a. (b) Owen, David. "Economy vs. Environment." *New Yorker*, 30 Mar. 2009, pp. 21-22. Accessed 5 Mar. 2020.
b. (c) Margonelli, Lisa. "Down and Dirty." *Atlantic Monthly*, May 2009, pp. 17-19.

2.8 Teacher check for correct bibliographical form and annotation.

2.9 Teacher check for correct bibliographical form and annotation.

2.10
a. Baker, David R. "$529 Million Loan for Plug-In Hybrids." *San Francisco Chronicle*, 23 Sept. 2009, p. A16. Accessed 18 Feb. 2020.
b. Grover, Paul. "Huge Frankfurt Goes Hybrid." *Melbourne Herald Sun*. 18 Sept. 2009, Sec. 1, p. 3.

c. Yap, Chuin. "Will China Tighten 'Rare Earth' Grip?" *Wall Street Journal, 3* Sept. 2009, p. C12.

2.11 Teacher check

2.12
a. Simon, Arthur R. *How Much is Enough?* Baker Books, 2003.
b. "People Already Care for the Needy— Without a Government Mandate." *USA Today*, 31 July 2009, p. A10.
c. Weber, Jeremy. "Desert Deaths." *Christianity Today*, Aug. 2009, pp. 8–9.
d. Catsoulis, Jeanette. "A Child's-Eye View of a Village That Subsists on Trash." *New York Times, 9* Sept. 2009, sec. 1, p. 9.
e. Sperling, Daniel and Deborah Gordon. *Two Billion Cars: Driving Toward Sustainability*. Oxford University Press, 2009.

2.13 Teacher check

2.14
a. paraphrase
b. summary
c. direct quotation
d. paraphrase
e. critical
f. summary

2.15 Teacher check
Notes should be primarily summary notes. Correct notecard form should be followed.

SELF TEST 2

2.01 Any order:
a. books
b. magazines
c. newspapers
d. essays
e. pamphlets

2.02 primary

2.03 Any order:
a. Dewey Decimal System
b. Library of Congress numbering system
c. Lettering system

2.04 primary source
2.05 tertiary source
2.06 secondary source
2.07 annotation
2.08 summary
2.09 plagiarism
2.010 false
2.011 true
2.012 false
2.013 false
2.014 false
2.015 false
2.016 false
2.017 true
2.018 false
2.019 false
2.020 incorrect
2.021 correct
2.022 incorrect
2.023 incorrect
2.024 incorrect
2.025 c
2.026 a
2.027 c
2.028 a
2.029 c
2.030 b
2.031 c
2.032 d

SECTION 3

3.1 a. Thesis change: Ability grouping in schools is detrimental to all students.
or discard notes 1 and 5

b. Thesis is stated in the negative. Should be changed to the positive.
Example: IQ tests are not the best way for testing intelligence, as they were once thought to be. All notes, except note 2, tell what IQ tests do measure. Note 2 should be discarded.

c. Discard notes 3 and 4. Leave thesis statement as it is.

3.2 Teacher check
The final thesis statement should pertain directly to the topic. It should be restricted, unified, and precise.

3.3 Teacher check
The three outline divisions should correspond to the notecard headings.

3.4 Example:

I. Introduction to School
   A. Nursery School Days
   B. Kindergarten
      1. Opening days
      2. Things I remember best
      3. "Graduation"

II. Elementary School
   A. First Grade Mysteries
      1. New surroundings
      2. New teacher
      3. New rules
      4. Schoolwork
      5. Getting used to the routine
         a. Cafeteria
         b. Assembly
         c. School bus
   B. Learning to Read
   C. Early Acquaintances
      1. The playground
      2. Friends and foes

3.5 Thesis statement: Behavior modification is an effective means to control weight.

I. Food
   A. Eating Habits
      1. Place
      2. Portions
      3. Water
      4. Plan
   B. Food Diary
      1. Kind of food
      2. Amount of food
      3. Place
      4. Time
      5. Cues
         a. Advertisement
         b. Past experiences

II. Exercise
   A. Exercise Habits
   B. Exercise Diary
      1. Time
      2. Amount
      3. Strenuous
         a. Jogging
         b. Jumping rope
         c. Walking

Thesis statement: Behavior modification is an effective means to control weight.

I. Food control is essential.
   A. Eating habits must be changed.
      1. Eat at a place where only eating is done.
      2. Eat half portions of food.
      3. Drink water with all food.
      4. Plan for large or high-calorie meals.
   B. A food diary must be kept.
      1. List the kind of food eaten.
      2. List the amount of food eaten.
      3. List the place the food was eaten.
      4. List the time the food was eaten.
      5. List any cues that caused unplanned eating.
         a. Advertising for food cues people to eat.
         b. Personal past experiences cue people to eat.

II. Exercise is essential.
   A. Usual exercise activity must be increased.
   B. An exercise activity diary must be kept.
      1. List the time of the exercise.
      2. List the amount of exercise.
      3. List strenuous exercise.
         a. Jogging is an excellent exercise.
         b. Jumping rope is excellent exercise.
         c. Walking is excellent exercise.

3.6　a. chronological
　　　b. sequential
　　　c. time

3.7　Teacher check
　　　Check the outline for proper form, divisions, subdivisions, and details.

3.8　The word *slang* is derived either from the past tense of *sling* or from *slanguage*. The *s* in *slanguage* comes from expressions such as *thieves' language*. Mario Pei, in his book *The Story of Lanugage*, says the term was first used in England in the middle eighteenth century. English literature slang, however, goes back to the sixteenth century. *Jargon*, applied especially to the vocabulary of a business or profession, and *cant*, an older term than *slang*, have come into relatively the same usage over the years.

3.9　Teacher check
　　　Check for paragraph development. A topic sentence, explanatory sentences, and details should be included.

3.10　Example:
　　　In addition to salaries, equipment that is used exclusively or nearly exclusively for the athletics program must be itemized. Equipment includes uniforms for athletes as well as for marching band, pompom line, cheerleaders, and any other group whose function is tied directly to the athletics program. Further, equipment includes balls, bats, nets, clubs, laundry and cleaning costs, first aid supplies and medical equipment (Smith 39). James Johnson cites another cost that could be included with equipment. It is the cost of utilities directly related to the sports program such as lighting for night football games and track meets, lighting and heating or air conditioning in the gymnasium, and transportation fees for team vans or buses (23).

3.11　a. citation
　　　b. citation
　　　c. no citation
　　　d. citation
　　　e. citation

3.12　Examples:
　　　a. For students to know the career opportunities in the near future, they must be exposed to career planning. Career planning will help students understand where their strengths and weaknesses are and where their talents lie. They will also learn which jobs require further schooling and how much those jobs will pay.
　　　b. Packing a backpack for a hike is quite a project. If the hike is overnight, the hiker needs a sleeping bag and a rubber pad as protection from the damp ground. Other essentials are a small stove for cooking the freeze-dried food and a mess kit to eat this packed food. Other essentials are matches, a first-aid kit, a canteen of water, and clean clothing.

3.13　a. The author does not care if anyone supports his idea.
　　　b. Fundamental skills are learned during childhood.
　　　c. Mr. Jones contends that there is life after death.
　　　　(Don't use first person.)
　　　d. A person should not jog immediately after eating a big meal.
　　　　(Don't use second person.)
　　　e. Jones and Smith disagree on taxation.
　　　　(no dialogue)

3.14　Teacher check
　　　Make suggestions to the student about form and content of the written draft. Be certain notes have been woven into the context of the paper.

3.15　a. topic with subtopics
　　　b. by the contrast
　　　c. uniforms

3.16　a. with an exclamation
　　　b. by the lights and people
　　　c. community education

3.17　a. with a short story
　　　b. the legend
　　　c. growing carnivorous plants

3.18 Teacher check
Be sure the introduction interests the reader
and gives an idea of the content of the
research paper.

3.19 a. yes
b. by the final statement
c. point forward

3.20 a. yes
b. with the words "as long as"
c. summarize

3.21 a. yes
b. the final sentence
c. expresses a hope

3.22 Teacher check
Check the conclusion to be sure it
summarizes or leaves the reader with a
thought. Be certain it does not appear
unnecessarily added.

3.23 Example:
The British and the Americans have
exchanged many slang words over the years.
British theater audiences who once needed a
printed glossary to understand an American
detective play now understand such slang
expressions as "tough guy," "lay off," "cop,"
and "oh, yeah." English police officers
sometimes hate to admit they understand
the vocabulary of British youth. Americans,
in turn, have borrowed such British slang as
"fed up" and "swank."

3.24 Teacher check
Check the research paper for obvious errors
in grammar and mechanics. Be sure that all
parts of the paper are easy to understand
and fully explained.

3.25 a. correct
b. incorrect
c. incorrect
d. correct
e. incorrect

3.26 Teacher check
Check the citations for correct form.

3.27 a. correct
b. incorrect
c. incorrect
d. incorrect
e. incorrect

3.28 Teacher check
Check the research paper for correct form.
Be certain all additional parts accompany
the paper. Check for content. Be certain all
areas are thoroughly developed and logically
presented.

SELF TEST 3

3.01 true
3.02 false
3.03 true
3.04 false
3.05 false
3.06 false
3.07 true
3.08 true
3.09 true
3.010 false
3.011 outline
3.012 details
3.013 logical progression
3.014 Any order:
a. time
b. sequence
c. chronology
3.015 Any order:
a. restricted
b. precise
c. unified
3.016 direct quotations
3.017 indirect quotations
3.018 citation
3.019 conclusion
3.020 transition
3.021 works cited page
3.022 correct
3.023 correct
3.024 incorrect
3.025 correct
3.026 incorrect
3.027 no
3.028 no
3.029 no
3.030 yes
3.031 no
3.032 correct
3.033 correct
3.034 incorrect
3.035 incorrect
3.036 yes
3.037 yes
3.038 no
3.039 yes
3.040 yes

LIFEPAC TEST

1. true
2. true
3. true
4. false
5. true
6. true
7. false
8. true
9. false
10. false
11. a
12. c
13. c
14. b
15. d
16. Any order
    a. summary
    b. paraphrase
    c. quotation
    d. critical
17. primary
18. outline
19. Any order:
    a. direct quotation
    b. summary of a discussion
    c. table
    d. writer's diagram from author's data
    or chart, diagram
20. b
21. g
22. d
23. f
24. i
25. a
26. h
27. j
28. k
29. e
30. c

ALTERNATE LIFEPAC TEST

1. true
2. true
3. false
4. false
5. false
6. true
7. false
8. true
9. true
10. false
11. c
12. a
13. d
14. c
15. b
16. a. direct quotation
    b. summary of a discussion
    c. table, chart, diagram
    d. writer's diagram from author's idea
17. the conclusion
18. plagiarism
19. primary
20. editorials or editorialized columns
21. i
22. g
23. d
24. k
25. h
26. j
27. b
28. a
29. c
30. f

LANGUAGE ARTS 1109

ALTERNATE LIFEPAC TEST

NAME _____

DATE _____

SCORE _____

78

97

Answer *true* **or** *false* (each answer, 2 points).

1. _____ The main body of the research paper should be written before writing the introduction.

2. _____ A firsthand source such as an interview would be a primary source.

3. _____ Giving credit for ideas which are not the student's own if they are included in the main body of the research paper is not necessary.

4. _____ The written guide the researcher uses in writing the research paper is called works cited.

5. _____ On the works cited page, the author's first name is written first.

6. _____ On the works cited page, a writer should indicate the date that an online source was accessed.

7. _____ At the top of the note card, the researcher should write the title of the book or article.

8. _____ A writer must include a citation for material which is directly quoted.

9. _____ Roman numerals in an outline signify main ideas.

10. _____ Each note card that the researcher prepares should contain as many ideas as possible.

Write the letter for the correct answer on the line (each answer, 3 points).

11. The final page of a research paper is called the _____ page.
    a. conclusion   b. outline   c. works cited   d. illustrative

12. The writer's thesis statement should include _____ .
    a. his purpose or intention for writing the paper
    b. a brief "thank you" to authors of material he has quoted
    c. a synopsis of the main body of the paper
    d. as many details, facts, and figures as possible

13. At the top of each note card, the researcher should write _____ .
    a. the note   b. the title of the source
    c. the call number   d. a general heading

14. Roman numerals in an outline signify _____ .
    a. details   b. subdivisions   c. main ideas   d. a general heading

15. The sentence that provides the theme of a research paper is called the _____ statement.
    a. primary   b. thesis   c. topic   d. lead

Complete these statements (each answer, 4 points).

16. Four kinds of information a writer *must* cite include a. _____ ,
    b. _____ , c. _____ , and d. _____ .

17. The summary at the end of a research paper is called _____ .

18. When a person does not give credit for another person's ideas, it is called

    _____ .

19. The original written work on a subject is called a _____ source.

20. The researcher should avoid using _____ as a resource because
    they are heavy with opinion and often void of fact.

Match these items (each answer, 3 points).

21. _____ bridge between thoughts

22. _____ note at the bottom of a bibliography card

23. _____ in-text citation

24. _____ library cataloguing method

25. _____ limited topic

26. _____ encyclopedia article

27. _____ method of ordering a research paper

28. _____ broad subject

29. _____ correct works cited entry

30. _____ summary

a. architecture

b. time

c. Hillenbrand, Laura. *Unbroken*. Random House, 2010.

d. "In a childhood of artful dodging, Louie made more than mischief " (Hillenbrand 3).

e. introduction

f. conclusion

g. annotation

h. three types of stairs

i. transition

j. general information source

k. Dewey Decimal System

LANGUAGE ARTS 1110

Unit 10: Reviewing Communication Skills and Literature

TEACHER NOTES

MATERIALS NEEDED FOR LIFEPAC	
Required	Suggested
• Auden, W.H. *"In Time of War,"* Modern Poetry. Maynard Mack, Leonard Dean, and William Frost, editors. Englewood Cliffs, NJ: Prentice-Hall, Inc., 1961 (or a similar anthology containing this poem).	• The entire Language Arts 1100 series for review • *"Annabel Lee"* by Edgar Allan Poe, or another poem containing examples of several metrical feet • *World Book Dictionary* or *American Heritage Dictionary* • Hemingway's *The Old Man and the Sea* or Language Arts LIFEPAC 1108 for Activities 4.97 and 4.98 • Wilder, Thornton. *Our Town.* • King James Version (KJV) of the Bible and/or other versions as permitted **Reference materials can be in printed, online, or digital formats.*

This four-part LIFEPAC is a complete summary of the nine individual LIFEPACs that compose the Language Arts 1100 series. Each of the four sections concentrates on a particular segment of the curriculum, beginning with the simple building blocks of words and going through sentences, essays, and papers, all the way to the American masterpieces of literature in novels, poetry, drama, and nonfiction. The activities of each section both review and reinforce the material covered in these summaries and also prepare the students for the sectional and LIFEPAC tests. Individual reading assignments include Ernest Hemingway's novel, *The Old Man and the Sea*; Thornton Wilder's play, *Our Town*; and a selection of various types of nonfiction and poetry.

EXTENDED WRITING ASSIGNMENT

Activity 4.98. This paper should reflect the student's ideas and opinions supported by evidence in the novel. In grading this composition, use the guidelines in this Teacher's Guide (1101) under the "Extended Writing Assignment" for mechanics and procedure. In this particular paper, go over the writing process that was discussed in the first three sections of this review and see if the students are using these techniques and properly organizing and developing their composition. Insertion of appositives and verbals, use of parallel construction, and construction of compound-complex sentences are some of the things to check for as well as punctuation or spelling.

ADDITIONAL LEARNING ACTIVITIES

Section 1: Analyzing Written Words

1. Have students use a thesaurus to look up any ten words and write down the synonyms.

2. Take these compiled lists of words and organize a discussion concerning the various levels of meaning for individual words. Include the two types of meaning (denotation and connotation).

3. Using either the novel *The Old Man and the Sea* or the play *Our Town*, go through chapters (or scenes) and pick out context clues that give hints about a character's nature, the author's meaning, or the theme of the work. Complete a couple examples as a class, and then have students make a list of several examples to share.

Section 2: Writing Effective Sentences

1. Go over a recently graded paper with each student, pointing out individual problems and trouble spots. Suggest ways to correct these errors in the future.

2. Choose several class essays (several good, several poorly written). Divide the class into groups of three or four. Give each group one essay to grade. Check to see if the student graders picked up their contemporaries' errors.

3. Let each student take the paper graded in the first activity in this section and rewrite that paper, attempting to correct all the original errors.

Section 3: Writing Expository Prose

1. Conduct a "brainstorming" session in class. Suggest several topics (religion, money, education, sports, etc.) and let the class take over, orally discussing the topics in order to develop first a controlling idea and then an analytical thesis.

2. Divide the class into small groups. Give each group a single topic and have them go to the library and check the subject headings in the library catalog for that topic. Have each group compile five or six bibliography cards on their topic.

3. Let each student choose one of the bibliography cards from the preceding activity and locate that source in the library. After skimming the book's index, the student should list several ideas that interest him and place them on 4" × 6" note cards in the proper format.

Section 4: Examining the Genres of American Literature

1. Using the text of *Our Town*, have the class go through the four basic steps of staging a play in the mind.

2. List seven major characters and state their relationships to each other.
   Answers provided:

   a. Emily — Webb's daughter, George's sweetheart and wife
   b. George — Gibbs's son, Emily's sweetheart and husband
   c. Mrs. Gibbs — George's mother and the doctor's wife
   d. Dr. Gibbs — town physician, George's father, Mrs. Gibbs's husband
   e. Mr. Webb — newspaper editor and Emily's father
   f. Mrs. Webb — Emily's mother and Mr. Webb's wife

g. Stage Manager — our guide and narrator for the play

Describe the setting of Act I.

Answer: The time is dawn, May 7, 1901, and the place is Grover's Corners, New Hampshire.

Locate clues in the dialogue about the characters.

Example answer: George and Emily's conversation in the drugstore reveals their true feelings toward each other.

3. Instruct students to capsulize several short key scenes from the play *Our Town* to express briefly the essential events and ideas in the play. The effect should resemble the collage technique used by artists. Have students present their skits.

4. Have students look up biographical information about one of the authors they have studied. Suggested authors include Willa Cather, Emily Dickinson, James Fenimore Cooper, and Jonathan Edwards.

5. Artistic students may want to sketch a picture of an author or a scene from one of the literary works studied in the Language Arts 1100 series.

6. Creative students may want to write a poem, a short dramatic scene, a short nonfiction essay, or a short fictional sketch.

Bible Memory Verses

Section 1
1 Thessalonians 4:18—comfort with words

Section 2
Psalm 17:2—sentence

Section 3
Job 19:23—writing words

Section 4
John 5:47—believing writings and words

Administer the LIFEPAC Test.

The test is to be administered in one session. Give no help except with directions.
Evaluate the tests and review areas where the students have done poorly.
Review the pages and activities that stress the concepts tested.
If necessary, administer the Alternate LIFEPAC Test.

ANSWER KEY

SECTION 1

1.1 through 1.3: Examples:
1.1 " ... by using context clues, the material around the new word that might suggest its meaning ... "
1.2 The climax, the turning point of a play, is always the most exciting part of the story.
1.3 The austere room, grim and poorly lighted, reflected the personality of the stern doctor.
1.4 Any order:
    a. if the word appears frequently and you wish to add it to your vocabulary
    b. if the context clues are inadequate
    c. if the surrounding words are unfamiliar
1.5 Either order:
    a. when explanatory material appears as a direct explanation, as an appositive
    b. when one or more synonyms restate the meaning of an unfamiliar word
1.6 Either order:
    a. direct explanation
    b. synonym
1.7 through 1.14: Examples:
1.7 a. hyperactive
    b. synonym
    c. polyester
    d. amphibian
    e. propel
1.8 a. bibliography
    b. democracy
    c. doxology
    d. geography
    e. microscope
1.9 a. beneficial
    b. companion
    c. submarine
    d. preparation
    e. senior
1.10 a. Pacific
    b. ambulatory
    c. vocal
    d. sequence
    e. fracture
1.11 a. hypodermic
    b. fracture
    c. hemoglobin
1.12 a. judicial
    b. mistrial
    c. abstain

1.13 a. democratic
    b. bureaucrat
    c. senate
1.14 a. microscope
    b. cosmic
    c. biology
1.15 b
1.16 g
1.17 a
1.18 i
1.19 j
1.20 c
1.21 h
1.22 e
1.23 Example:
Large amounts of data were accumulated, sifted, and then assembled into a whole. Some words were included immediately (in space and technology, especially). Others were added after they had been in use for some time.
1.24 Any order:
    a. Dr. Samuel Johnson's
    b. Noah Webster's
    c. *Oxford English Dictionary*
1.25 a. the history of a word
    b. the writing or making of dictionaries
    c. *Oxford English Dictionary* of 12 volumes; complete; considered the ultimate authority of the English language
1.26 Examples:
essays about language, business letters, addresses of colleges
1.27 false
1.28 true
1.29 false
1.30 c
1.31 a
1.32 b
1.33 d
1.34 f
1.35 a. a list of sources of information about a certain subject with critical or explanatory notes
    b. a special dictionary of synonyms and antonyms
    c. not shortened or condensed; complete

SELF TEST 1

1.01   i
1.02   a
1.03   c
1.04   g
1.05   h
1.06   d
1.07   b
1.08   e
1.09   false
1.010 true
1.011 true
1.012 false
1.013 true
1.014 *OED*
1.015 the context clues
1.016 historical method
1.017 *Roget's Thesaurus*
1.018 Any order:
   a. to provide information about words
   b. to standardize the language
   c. to offer supplemental, miscellaneous information—charts, copyreading information, essays on history and structure of language
1.019 Any order:
   a. Dr. Samuel Johnson's
   b. Noah Webster's
   c. *OED*
1.020 Any order:
   a. legal
   b. medical
   c. scientific

SECTION 2

2.1   Example:
My brother and I learned a new song, we were invited to sing at a special program at our church.
2.2   Example:
My tennis game is not very good; however, I can beat almost anyone at ping pong.
2.3   S
2.4   C
2.5   C
2.6   The boy who has dark red hair and sits in the front row did well on the test.
2.7   Since you've been gone, I've finished the book.
2.8   I read the book that you recommended.
2.9   Any order:
   a. who
   b. which
   c. that
   d. whoever
   e. what
   f. whichever
2.10 Any order:
   a. because
   b. since
   c. although
   d. where
   e. as
   f. when
2.11 Example:
Whenever the alarm goes off, our school has a fire drill.
2.12 through 2.15: Examples:
2.12 a sentence containing one main/independent clause
2.13 a sentence containing two or more main/independent clauses
2.14 a sentence containing one main/independent clause and one or more subordinate/dependent clauses
2.15 a sentence containing two or more main/independent clauses and one or more subordinate/dependent clauses
2.16 Whoever is tallest should put the books away; S
2.17 Do whatever task needs to be done; O
2.18 Give the book to whomever is next on the list; OP
2.19 The best book is that one on the table; SC
2.20 Whoever wants to go to the football game must buy a ticket; N

2.21 The cat <u>that is sitting in the window</u> weighs twenty-six pounds; Adj.

2.22 The acolyte <u>who has the dark hair</u> is Mrs. Howard's oldest son; Adj.

2.23 Examples:
  a. We will eat whatever you order.
  b. My jacket was the one that was torn.
  c. Since I have a test tomorrow, I need to study.

2.24 Any order; examples:
  a. simple: The cat drank the milk from the saucer.
  b. compound: The wind blew, and the boat sailed across the lake.
  c. complex: The horse that won the last race was the gray mare.
  d. compound-complex: The boy who delivers our newspaper was sick and his father took over the route.

2.25 Any order:
  a. noun
  b. adjective
  c. adverb

2.26 <u>Jogging daily</u> is good for your health; S

2.27 I am tired of <u>studying for this test</u>; OP

2.28 Preparation for <u>writing a paper</u> should include taking notes; UP

2.29 My favorite pastime is <u>playing golf</u>; PN

2.30 a. playing   b. played

2.31 a. working   b. worked

2.32 a. jumping   b. jumped

2.33 a. talking   b. talked

2.34 Examples:
  a. The girl throwing the ball is the best pitcher on the team.
  b. The little dog left by the side of the road was found by Jeff.

2.35 Example:
  To win a marathon race is my goal.

2.36 Example:
  I have always wanted to go to Mexico.

2.37 Any order:
  a. gerund
  b. infinitive
  c. participle

2.38 Example:
  a. My brother, Jerry, is now going to college.
  b. My friend, the girl from the city, visited me yesterday.

2.39 Mr. Smith

2.40 novel

2.41 We

2.42 GP

2.43 PP

2.44 PP

2.45 IP

2.46 through 2.48: Examples:

2.46 The dog with the rhinestone collar was barking fiercely.

2.47 The project should be finished in two weeks.

2.48 At the end of the play the audience gave the cast a ten-minute standing ovation.

2.49 My two goals are to run an eight-minute mile and to place first.
  or
  My two goals are running an eight-minute mile and placing first.

2.50 He ran down the steps, jumped in his car, and drove off quickly.

2.51 He had marked in red ink on the map the places we were to watch for.

2.52 The electrician said he would repair the light Wednesday.

2.53 The man wearing a bandanna leaned against the building.

2.54 *They* is vague. Replace it with a noun.

2.55 Change *us* to *our*, the possessive case.

2.56 Change *I* to *me*, objective case.

2.57 Change *me* to *I*, nominative case.

SELF TEST 2

2.01	k
2.02	h
2.03	i
2.04	a
2.05	g
2.06	c
2.07	b
2.08	e
2.09	f
2.010	d
2.011	false
2.012	true
2.013	false
2.014	false
2.015	true
2.016	true
2.017	true
2.018	false
2.019	noun
2.020	dependent
2.021	comma
2.022	predicate nominative
2.023	relative pronoun
2.024	morpheme
2.025	thesaurus

2.026 Any order:
   a. gerunds
   b. participles
   c. infinitives

2.027 Either order:
   a. adjective
   b. adverb

2.028 Any order:
   a. noun
   b. adverb
   c. adjective

2.029 Any order:
   a. to provide information about words
   b. to standardize the language
   c. to offer supplemental, miscellaneous information—charts, copyreading information, essays on history and structure of language

SECTION 3

3.1 through 3.3: Examples:

3.1   A religion is the importance of belief in God.

3.2   Belief in God is very important.

3.3   Belief in God is important because that belief strengthens a person's character, strengthens the family unit, and strengthens society and the world community.

3.4   Teacher check

3.5   true

3.6   true

3.7   false

3.8   false

3.9   true

3.10   Type or carefully handwrite the paper; use good quality white paper (standard size); leave margins 1-1½" and double space.

3.11   title page (or cover page); outline page (if requested); text

3.12   proofread it

3.13   a. have it evaluated by an expert (teacher)
           b. learn to evaluate your own writing
           c. do more writing

3.14   Teacher check

3.15   outside sources

3.16   working bibliography

3.17   EBSCO host or an online periodical database

3.18   Any order:
           a. decide on a limited topic
           b. brainstorm (if necessary, add information by using a general source, such as an encyclopedia)
           c. prepare a working outline
           d. obtain a list of potential sources of information and set each up on a bibliography card

3.19   false

3.20   true

3.21   true

3.22   parenthesis

3.23   a listing of sources

3.24   central idea

3.25   analytical

3.26   3 × 5

3.27   4 × 6

3.28   Either order:
           a. themes of character
           b. themes of ideas

3.29   Any order:
           a. what the character says
           b. what the character does
           c. what other characters say about them
           d. what the author says about them

3.30	exposition
3.31	theme
3.32	an allegory
3.33	false
3.34	false
3.35	false
3.36	false
3.37	Teacher check

SELF TEST 3

3.01 h

3.02 g

3.03 j

3.04 c

3.05 f

3.06 d

3.07 e

3.08 a

3.09 k

3.010 b

3.011 true

3.012 false

3.013 true

3.014 true

3.015 true

3.016 standardizes the language

3.017 a dictionary of synonyms and antonyms

3.018 subordinate clause

3.019 collected at the end of the paper or on the works cited page

3.020 thesis statement

3.021 Any order:
   a. simple
   b. compound
   c. complex
   d. compound-complex

3.022 Any order:
   a. by what the character says
   b. by what the character does
   c. by what other characters say about the character
   d. by what the author says about the character

3.023 Examples; any order:
   a. a library catalog search
   b. an online search engine/EBSCO
   c. textbooks
   d. vertical files
   e. specialized indexes
   f. bibliographies

3.024 Any order:
   a. exposition
   b. narration
   c. description
   d. persuasion or argumentation

3.025 Either order:
   a. theme of character analysis
   b. theme of ideas

3.026 Any order:
   a. gerund
   b. participle
   c. infinitive

3.027 Any order:
a. adjective
b. adverb
c. noun (appositive)

3.028 Any order:
a. footnotes or endnotes
b. bibliography
c. supporting material (or quotes)

SECTION 4

4.1 primitive religious rites

4.2 a. tragedy
b. comedy

4.3 William Shakespeare

4.4 a. sixteenth
b. seventeenth

4.5 true

4.6 false

4.7 false

4.8 true

4.9 The influence of Puritans opposed drama. There were no funds for theater, no established audiences, and old prejudice connected theater to immorality of royalty.

4.10 a. romantic literary—an imitation of classical drama
b. realistic vernacular—comedy of American material

4.11 Any order:
a. established audience
b. competent actors
c. physical resources to stage plays
d. revival of drama in Europe
e. growth of "little theater" in America

4.12 Any order:
a. Broadway
b. legitimate theater
c. motion pictures
d. television
e. university theater
f. little theater
g. regional theater
h. repertory theater

4.13 Any order:
a. expressionism
b. realism
c. symbolism

4.14 Any order:
a. movement toward realism
b. using serious problems as plays' subjects
c. favoring symbolism in playwriting

4.15 theme

4.16 stage directions

4.17 setting

4.18 a. static
b. dynamic

4.19 plot

4.20 Any order:
a. reflects life
b. criticizes life
c. interprets life

4.21 Any order:
  a. explore the human condition
  b. examine moral and social problems and man's values
  c. dramatize a wide variety of human experiences

4.22 a. *The Bridge of San Luis Rey*
  (b-c: Either order:)
  b. *Our Town*
  c. *The Skin of our Teeth*

4.23 simplicity

4.24 universal

4.25 Example:
  to be aware of life, each minute, each day—take good heed to the living

4.26 c

4.27 b

4.28 d

4.29 f

4.30 g

4.31 a

4.32 Any order:
  a. unique form
  b. language
  c. rhythm
  d. compressed meaning

4.33 stanza or verse

4.34 Either order:
  a. rhyme
  b. imagery

4.35 rhythm

4.36 compressed meaning

4.37 Teacher check

4.38 a. Déep iňtó thăt dárkňess péariňg; trochea
  b. Mў lóve ĭs líke a réd, rĕd róse; iamb
  c. Ĭt was máňy aňd máňy a yéar ăgó; anapest

4.39 a. device for measuring the sound of poetry
  b. a three-syllable foot with stressed syllable first, followed by two unaccented ones

4.40 Teacher check

4.41 c

4.42 d

4.43 e

4.44 b

4.45 a

4.46 a. alliteration—repetition within a line of initial consonant sounds
  b. onomatopoeia—words imitating the sound of a specific thing
  c. consonance—use of corresponding consonant sounds in a line
  d. assonance—use of corresponding vowel sounds in a line

4.47 form

4.48 blank verse

4.49 Walt Whitman

4.50 narrative

4.51 lyric

4.52 Any order:
  a. simile—saying one thing is like another
  b. metaphor—stating directly that one thing is another
  c. personification—giving nonliving things human characteristics

4.53 a. Bryant says that Cole will take a living picture in his heart—a picture such as one he has painted.
  b. Examples:
  "lone lakes," "rocks rich," "solemn streams," "bloom ... blaze," etc.

4.54 connotations

4.55 compressed meanings

4.56 Any order:
  a. faith
  b. hope
  c. love

4.57 man-centered faith

4.58 "Song of Myself"

4.59 Any order:
  a. Longfellow
  b. Auden
  c. Eliot

4.60 b

4.61 e

4.62 c

4.63 a

4.64 b

4.65 c

4.66 a

4.67 Nathaniel Hawthorne

4.68 Herman Melville

4.69 James Fenimore Cooper

4.70 *The Spy*

4.71 *The Scarlet Letter*

4.72 introducing new territories for writers to explore

4.73 *Moby Dick*

4.74 c

4.75 d

4.76 a

4.77 e

4.78 false

4.79 false

4.80 true

4.81 true

4.82 false

4.83 b

4.84 a

4.85 c

4.86 a

4.87 c

4.88 Examples; any order:
  a. detective
  b. political
  c. psychological
  f. regional
  e. historical
  f. naturalistic

4.89 climax

4.90 exposition

4.91 mood

4.92 Any order:
  a. plot
  b. characterization
  c. mood

4.93 b

4.94 e

4.95 a

4.96 c

4.97 Teacher check

4.98 Teacher check

4.99 Any order:
  a. newspaper stories
  b. magazine articles
  c. letters
  d. formal essays
  e. informal essays
  f. diaries
  g. journals
  h. biographies

4.100 a form of prose that explains or expresses certain ideas and information that is truthful

4.101 a. Fiction is imaginary/nonfiction is real and based on fact.
  b. Fiction is to entertain/nonfiction is to inform or instruct.
  c. Fiction is narrative prose/nonfiction is basically expository or descriptive.

4.102 propaganda

4.103 Either order:
  a. more education
  b. more leisure time

4.104 electronic or digital

4.105 Any order:
  a. clarity
  b. unity
  c. completeness

4.106 Any order:
  a. illustrative, using details, examples, definitions or comparisons
  b. analytical, breaking a subject down into parts and showing relations to the whole
  c. argumentative, trying to convince someone of a particular viewpoint

4.107 c

4.108 d

4.109 c

4.110 Both compare two unlike things but a simile uses *as* or *like* while a metaphor compares the two directly.

4.111 Francis Bacon

4.112 an attempt

4.113 Either order:
  a. Joseph Addison
  b. Richard Steele

4.114 A formal essay has a serious tone, precise style, and an instructive purpose. An informal one has a conversational tone, casual style, and an entertaining purpose.

4.115 false

4.116 true

4.117 true

4.118 false

4.119 true

4.120 b

4.121 e

4.122 a

4.123 They give us information about important people in history and help us to understand the times they lived in.

4.124 autobiography

4.125 Either order:
  a. magazines
  b. newspapers

4.126 specialty

4.127 *Reader's Digest*

4.128 editorial

4.129 Any order:
  a. who
  b. what
  c. where
  d. when
  e. how

4.130 Any order:
  a. ideas
  b. humor
  c. personal experience
  d. biography and autobiography

SELF TEST 4

4.01	j
4.02	i
4.03	b
4.04	l
4.05	a
4.06	p
4.07	d
4.08	g
4.09	c
4.010	m
4.011	h
4.012	f
4.013	n
4.014	q
4.015	o
4.016	k
4.017	plot
4.018	*Everyman*
4.019	clarity
4.020	James Fenimore Cooper
4.021	*A True Relation*
4.022	context clues
4.023	Grover's Corners, N.H.
4.024	*Uncle Tom's Cabin*
4.025	William Dean Howells

4.026 Any order:
- a. faith
- b. hope
- c. love

4.027 Either order:
- a. relative pronoun
- b. subordinate conjunction

4.028 Walt Whitman

4.029 iambic pentameter

4.030 climax

4.031 Either order:
- a. Mark Twain
- b. Henry James

4.032	true
4.033	false
4.034	true
4.035	false
4.036	false
4.037	true
4.038	false
4.039	false
4.040	false
4.041	true

4.042 Any order:
- a. Fiction is imaginary while nonfiction is based on fact.
- b. Fiction is narrative prose but nonfiction is exposition and description and rarely just narrative.
- c. Fiction's purpose is to entertain, nonfiction's purpose is to inform and instruct.

4.043 Any order:
- a. participle phrase—functions as an adjective
- b. gerund phrase—functions as a noun
- c. infinitive phrase—functions as a noun, adjective, or adverb

4.044 Any order:
- a. exposition
- b. incident
- c. rising action
- d. climax
- e. falling action
- f. resolution

4.045 Any order:
- a. illustrative—*The Federalist Papers*
- b. analytical—*Walden*
- c. argumentative—Paul's defense of Christianity

4.046
- a. Líttlĕ Lámb, whŏ máde thĕe?
- b. trochee
- c. Thĕ leáves arĕ fállĭng, brówn ănd góld.
- d. iamb

4.047 Any order:
- a. nature-centered faith, "Thanatopsis"
- b. man-centered faith, "Song of Myself"
- c. God-centered faith, "Psalm of Life"

4.048 Any order:
- a. supporting quotes within the text
- b. footnotes or end notes
- c. bibliography

4.049 Any order:
- a. plot
- b. characterization
- c. mood

4.050 "Take good heed to the living." Emily realizes this when she returns to life in the third act and sees that the living fail to appreciate life because they're too busy. Thus, Wilder directly states his moral in the play's dialogue through Emily.

4.051 Any order:
- a. simple, one main clause only
- b. compound, two main or independent clauses
- c. complex, one main clause and one or more subordinate (dependent) clauses
- d. compound-complex, two or more main clauses and one or more subordinate clauses

4.052 Any order:
- a. newspapers
- b. magazine articles
- c. biographies and autobiographies
- d. letters
- e. diaries
- f. journals
- g. formal essays
- h. informal essays

4.053 Any order:
- a. irony
- b. images
- c. symbols
- d. allegory

4.054 Any order:
- a. Dr. Samuel Johnson's
- b. Noah Webster's
- c. Oxford University's

4.055 Any order:
- a. James Fenimore Cooper
- b. Nathaniel Hawthorne
- c. Herman Melville

4.056 Either order:
- a. standard
- b. nonstandard

4.057 Any order:
- a. atmosphere
- b. setting
- c. tone

LIFEPAC TEST

1.	l	**44.**	Any order:
2.	j		a. plot
3.	o		b. characterization
4.	k		c. mood
5.	m	**45.**	citations
6.	i	**46.**	Either order:
7.	n		a. exposition
8.	d		b. description
9.	a	**47.**	adjective
10.	c	**48.**	Any order:
11.	f		a. realism
12.	h		b. symbolism
13.	e		c. expressionism
14.	g	**49.**	independent
15.	b	**50.**	Any order:
16.	true		a. the illustrative pattern
17.	true		b. the analytical pattern
18.	false		c. the argumentative pattern
19.	true		
20.	true		
21.	true		
22.	true		
23.	true		
24.	false		
25.	false		
26.	b		
27.	a		
28.	b		
29.	a		
30.	c		
31.	d		
32.	a		
33.	c		
34.	c		
35.	b		
36.	d		
37.	c		
38.	bibliography		
39.	personification		
40.	nominative		
41.	a. Cooper		
	b. Melville		
	c. Hawthorne		
42.	Any order:		
	a. faith		
	b. hope		
	c. love		
43.	sentence		

ALTERNATE LIFEPAC TEST

1. g
2. i
3. h
4. k
5. l
6. j
7. n
8. a
9. c
10. d
11. e
12. o
13. p
14. f
15. b
16. true
17. true
18. false
19. false
20. false
21. true
22. true
23. false
24. true
25. true
26. b
27. a
28. c
29. b
30. d
31. a
32. d
33. a
34. b
35. c
36. d
37. c
38. Any order:
    a. faith
    b. hope
    c. love
39. Either order:
    a. topic
    b. sentence
40. Any order:
    a. standard English
    b. objective attitude toward subject
    c. omission of contractions

41. Any order:
    a. roots
    b. prefixes
    c. suffixes
42. hyperbole
43. infinitive
    or verbal
44. parallel construction
45. nineteenth
46. Any order:
    a. plot
    b. characterization
    c. mood
47. *Pilgrim's Progress*
48. Any order:
    a. expressionism
    b. realism
    c. symbolism
49. Either order:
    a. exposition
    b. description
50. Either order:
    a. synonyms
    b. antonyms
51. Any order:
    a. analytical
    b. illustrative
    c. argumentative
52. *The Scarlet Letter*

LANGUAGE ARTS 1110
ALTERNATE LIFEPAC TEST

87
109

NAME _____

DATE _____

SCORE _____

Match these items (each answer, 1 point).

1. _____ metaphor
2. _____ autobiography
3. _____ adjective clause
4. _____ Henry Wadsworth Longfellow
5. _____ bibliography
6. _____ *The Scarlet Letter*
7. _____ The number one best seller of the nineteenth century
8. _____ independent clause
9. _____ image
10. _____ pioneer of free verse in poetry
11. _____ William Hill Brown
12. _____ personification
13. _____ Thornton Wilder
14. _____ Samuel Johnson
15. _____ the Stage Manager

a. a main clause that can function as a sentence
b. guide and narrator for *Our Town*
c. a word picture with a concrete reference in the real world
d. Walt Whitman
e. *The Power of Sympathy*
f. first person to use historical method of dictionary research
g. a direct comparison
h. clause modifying a noun or pronoun
i. story of an author's own life
j. a novel by Nathaniel Hawthorne
k. a religious poet in the early nineteenth century
l. a listing of sources used in a paper
m. Edgar Allan Poe
n. Harriet Beecher Stowe's *Uncle Tom's Cabin*
o. giving an inanimate object human characteristics
p. author of *Our Town*

Answer *true* **or** *false* (each answer, 1 point).

16. _____ EBSCO host is an online magazine and newspaper database.

17. _____ The first book written in America was John Smith's *A True Relation*.

18. _____ A joining word in a sentence is the topic sentence.

19. _____ *Everyman* is a famous morality play of the Renaissance.

20. _____ An appositive functions like an adverb in a given sentence.

21. _____ A paraphrase is using your own words to express someone else's ideas.

22. _____ The *OED* is a twenty-volume unabridged reference work.

23. _____ Slang is a form of standard English.

24. _____ Plagiarism is stealing someone else's ideas or words without giving that person credit.

25. _____ The nominative case of a pronoun is used as the subject of a sentence or clause.

Write the letter for the correct answer on the line (each answer, 2 points).

26. The turning point of a play or novel is its _____ .
    a. plot   b. climax   c. characterization   d. setting

27. The controlling idea of a paper or a essay is its _____ .
    a. thesis   b. topic sentence   c. transition   d. paraphrase

28. Specific notations in a paper that refer a reader to a specific page and author of their source

    of material are _____ .
    a. verbals   b. plagiarism   c. citations   d. etymology

29. The *Oxford English Dictionary* is most helpful in researching the _____ development of a word.
    a. figurative   b. etymological   c. descriptive   d. symbolistic

30. The central idea of any given paragraph is its _____ .
    a. image   b. transition   c. outline   d. topic sentence

31. The most reliable method of research in lexicography is the _____ method.
    a. historical   b. mechanical
    c. expository   d. scientific

32. When you use criticism about a literary work in a paper, that criticism is a _____ source.
    a. standard   b. primary   c. basic   d. secondary

33. The smallest unit of meaning in a word is a _____ .
    a. morpheme   b. hyperbole   c. verbal   d. conjunction

34. Like the verb, a gerund in a sentence may take a(n) _____ .
    a. subject   b. object   c. clause   d. phrase

35. Using synonyms in a sentence to restate or clarify the meaning of an unfamiliar word is an example of a _____ .
    a. transition   b. paraphrase   c. context clue   d. subordinate clause

36. An introductory adverb clause is usually followed by a _____ .
    a. semicolon   b. colon   c. period   d. comma

37. The correct pattern for a simple sentences _____ .
    a. SV;SV   b. SS; and SV   c. SV   d. SS

Complete these statements (each answer, 2 points).

38. List the three universal human experiences American poets have chosen as the subjects of their poems.

    a. _____

    b. _____

    c. _____

39. The two types of outlines used in writing a paper are a. _____ and

    b. _____ .

40. Three formal requirements for writing expository prose are a. _____ ,

    b. _____ , and c. _____ .

41. A knowledge of Greek and Latin a. _____ , b. _____ ,

    and c. _____ will help to expand your vocabulary.

42. The use of exaggerated language in descriptive writing is _____ .

43. The phrase *to run* is an example of a(n) _____ .

44. The sentence construction, "Thine is the kingdom and the power and the glory," is an example of a(n) _____ .

45. Cooper, Melville, and Hawthorne were the three great American novelists of the early _____ century.

46. All novels have three basic elements in common. They are a. _____ ,

    b. _____ , and c. _____ .

47. A famous example of a fictional work that is a complete allegory is _____
    _____ .

48. The three schools of playwriting that developed in America in the twentieth century are
    a. _____ , b. _____ , and
    c. _____ .

49. Nonfiction uses two basic forms of writing: a. _____ and
    b. _____ .

50. *Roget's Thesaurus* is a dictionary of a. _____ and
    b. _____ .

51. All expository writing can be divided into three major patterns of composition. They are
    a. _____ , b. _____ , and
    c. _____ .

52. Probably the most famous symbol in American literature is _____ .